T0130126

COSTA RICA: THE PURA VIDA COUNTRY

JOHN P. CROSS

COSTA RICA: THE PURA VIDA COUNTRY
A TRAVEL GUIDE

iUniverse books may be ordered through booksellers or by contacting:

iUniverse
1663 Liberty Drive
Bloomington, IN 47403
www.iuniverse.com
1-800-Authors (1-800-288-4677)

ISBN: 978-1-5320-9378-4 (sc)
ISBN: 978-1-5320-9379-1 (e)

Library of Congress Control Number: 2020902885

Print information available on the last page.

iUniverse rev. date: 02/28/2020

"A journey of a thousand miles must begin with a single step."
-Lao Tzu

Dedicated to

Dr. Edward H. Mosley,
Emeritus Latin America History,
University of Alabama.

Dr. Mosley was dedicated to his study of Latin America. He would say in his classes "There is more than one America. In the United States we are one member of the Americas!" There is North America, Mexico, Central America and South America. America is a member of a larger community diverse in language, history, and culture. We are all Americans.

Give back to the environment. Sustainability is the goal. We have only one planet and we must preserve it. Vaya con dios amigos y amigas! And Pura Vida!

John P. Cross
Atlanta, USA

Contents

Preface

"When you look like your passport
photo, it is time to go home."
-Erma Bombeck

Travelers today are increasingly becoming interested in ecotourism travel in exotic locations. Costa Rica is probably the most popular destination to please the ecotourism traveler. It has rain forests, volcanoes, great trekking, zip lining, rafting and beautiful beaches. There is a variety of monkeys, sloth, frogs, butterflies, and birds located in a variety of national parks dedicated to ecotourism, and sustainability. My book is designed to get the traveler close to nature. The goal is designed to save you money on your trip if you are willing to budget your trip. It could be restaurants, or the hotel, or hostel. Also, day trips.

In the Appendices you will find an extensive bibliography for a reference and further reading. It is my source material. The book along with my travel has been completely researched. May you benefit from this. There is a packing checklist with items to pack. But do not overpack. Much of it depends upon the climate at your destination. For the modern traveler there is the use of computer apps, or how to use the mobile device on a trip when planning. Next, there is a mini Spanish dictionary for a quick reference. I also included "slang" language from Costa Rica. A theme of this book is budget travel. How to travel without breaking the bank. This book is a complete travel guide. Costa Rica from A to Z. May you benefit from my travel experiences. This book promotes ecotourism to travel wisely. Remember as chief Seattle said, "Leave only footprints." One must respect the flora and the animals, and the people and their culture. And always

"Travel is fatal to prejudice, bigotry, and narrow-mindedness, and many of our people need it sorely on these accounts. Broad, wholesome, charitable views of men and things cannot be acquired by vegetating in one little corner of the earth all one's lifetime."
-Mark Twain

Chapter 1

Ecotourism and Biodiversity

"We live in a wonderful world that is full of
beauty, charm and adventure. There is no
end to the adventures we can have if only
we seek them with our eyes open."
-Jawaharlal Nehru

Ecotourism and biodiversity have become popular with
travelers today. Ecotourism is a major reason Costa
Rica is growing in popularity. Costa Rica has made a
major commitment to national parks, and protecting
its animals, and flora and fauna. At one time in history
coffee and bananas drove the economy. The tourist boom
in ecotourism now drives the economy. Tourists flock
to see the rainforest, oceans, mountains and wildlife.
Tourists want to get close to nature. It can happen in
Costa Rica!

Growth of tourism. Tourism took off in the 1980s, Coinciding with the worldwide growth of interest and concern of environmentalism, biodiversity, and ecology. Costa Rica was a natural for the development of this type of travel. All the elements were there. The rest is history. The major reason why the traveler goes to Costa Rica is to experience the adventure of the biodiversity of the landscape, the many bird species, lots of mammals such as the sloth and monkeys. And don't forget the frogs. There is an incredible diversity of plants. The goal of ecotourism is to maintain sustainability of the various species. I am sorry to report that the efforts failed in 1989 when mysteriously in the Monteverde cloud forest the beautiful golden toad disappeared from our planet and was not to be seen again. No one is sure why the Golden frog disappeared. One theory is because of climate change there has been an increase in toxins and pollutants which entered the frogs body system. Another is the UV light levels have become too dangerous for their sensitive skins. Regardless, the Golden frog disappeared. Never to return. The people and government of Costa Rica are dedicated to preserving the natural environment. They are dedicated to maintaining their extensive natural park systems. It is an excellent place to learn about biodiversity. Just go hiking in the rain forest or take a zip line.

What is ecotourism? It is the practice of touring natural habits in a manner meant to minimize ecolgical impact while benefiting the local people, Merriam Webster. It is responsible travel to natural areas that conserves the environment, sustain the well-being of the local people, and involves education. Ties, 2015. The goal is sustainable tourism, so that both the tourist and local people benefit.

"Leave only footprints."-Chief

Chapter 2

A Brief History of Costa Rica

"The world is a book those who do
not travel read only one page."
-St. Augustine

A brief history of Costa Rica. Most history books of Costa Rica begin with 1502, when Christopher Columbus, the great navigator, arrived in Puerto Limon, on the Caribbean side. The first Europeans now had arrived, and they become a part of the Americas. The cultural impact of the Spanish would change life in the future. The life of indigenous natives such as the BriBri tribes was to be changed forever. The Spanish always left their indelible cultural impact wherever they settled. Molina, The History of Costa Rica page 20-23.

After going ashore, Columbus named the country Costa Rica, or "the rich coast" because he had discovered a country rich in gold and silver. But he was wrong. Costa Rica got what income it had in the future because of cattle, coffee, bananas and by the late 1980s and 1990s ecotourism. But there were hurdles along the way. The first permanent Settlement was Cartago, by Coronado. Cartago was the first capital. By 1562 this Spanish colonist had moved inland to the Central Valley and founded Cartago, The first colonial capital. The Valley was Brown for its hospitable climate and fertile soil for farming. In 1737 San Jose was founded. In 1823 San Jose was made the official capital following the independence of Costa Rica from Spain. Next came the attempted takeover by William Walker, a mercenary from the USA in 1856. He declared himself president of Costa Rica. He had hired his own army to take control of the country. Walker and his mercenaries were defeated in 1856. Walker was forced to give up and leave Costa Rica. Later in 1860 he tried again to make himself president but failed to get rid of him once and for all he was executed by a firing squad. A national hero emerged from the conflict, Juan Santa Maria. Santa Maria was a humble farm laborer who led a volunteer army to eject Walker. Molina writes Santa Maria "turned the tide of battle of Rivas in favor of Costa Rican troops."

Walkers defeat in SJO.

Santamaria set fire to a building occupied by walkers' troops in a surprise attack. The troops of Walkers were defeated. Walker was forced to leave Costa Rica and told to never return. This was 1856.

As a result, the national hero of Costa Rica became Santamaria, although he was killed in the attack. Thus, begins the legend of the "Little drummer boy." Molina, page 67-68. The International Airport of San Jose (SJO) is named for Juan Santa Maria. Liberia is the home of the other major airport. It is closer to the Pacific, and El Coco near Tamarindo.

Next came the banana man, Sam Zemurray, A Jewish immigrant from Russia, came to the USA in the late 19th century. He settled in Alabama because he had friends there. See the book Cohen, The fish that 8 the whales. He was fascinated by bananas, and he eventually became president of United fruit company. But before he had to go through a process. He was sort of a vaga bond peddler of bananas. He was a businessman who was driven by the desire to be successful as an immigrant. His legacy would be bananas from Central America. Sam was associated with the port of mobile and later New Orleans. Sam the entrepreneur, collected discarded bananas from the docks. From there he sold them to customers. There was a profit to be made and Sam made that profit. By 1878 there was a thriving population of bananas to New Orleans. Sam was there to take advantage of the trade. From fruit peddler to international businessman. A risk taker. He had contracts in Honduras in Costa Rica he died in 1961. Sam built a luxury antebellum style home on St. Charles Ave in New Orleans. Near Tulane university. He favored Tulane university. Where he had many contracts. Today the home is the official home of the president of Tulane university. His Daughter still lives in Uptown New Orleans. By 1907, New Orleans was the nation's largest banana importer. Sam "the banana man" Was the reason why. A man who went from a small-town banana peddler to international businessman. He ran the biggest fruit company. Dreams can come true. Sam was known for his charitable donations. He gave a lot back to society. Later in life, in New Orleans, at Brennan's restaurant I enjoyed the banana foster. It was made from rum, sugar, bananas from Costa Rica. Thank you, Sam, or "Mr. Z".

The Coffee Boom 1840's

The 1840's Saw the growth of coffee as an agricultural produce in the fertile Central Valley. The demand and exports for coffee increased from the USA in Europe. It was called the Golden grain. At last the rich discovery had happened. Even the small farmers benefited.

Bananas 1870's

Bananas were the "yellow gold." The export of bananas was made possible by the constitution of The Atlantic railroad from the Central Valley to the Caribbean, and the port of Limon. This would make it easier to reach the markets in the USA and Europe. The funding of the project was made by a US citizen, Minor C. Keith. Eventually this became the United fruit company. They grew bananas to feed the railroad workers. A new industry was underway. Costa Rica became the world's largest exporter of bananas. By 1878, the ports of Mobile and New Orleans received their imports of bananas from Costa Rica. Later refrigerated ships were used to prevent spoilage. Consumers went crazy for this yellow fruit. In 1949 the government of Costa Rica approved a landmark decision by abolishing the military in a new constitution. This followed the civil war. The citizens were tired of the meddling of the military into politics. The new constitution called for desegregation and gave women the right to vote. A new nation was emerging.

Quakers

In 1949, pacifist Quakers From Alabama, decided to move to Costa Rica. They moved to Monteverde, which means Green Mountains. The Reason was because they were pacifists, and Costa Rica Had abolished their military. The USA was entering the Korean War. They wanted no part of the war. Also, the Costa Rican's offered them sanctuary on Mount Verde. The Quakers became the first Conservationists in Costa Rica. They were farmers and dairy people. They were the first protectors of the damage to the environment. Now they protect their dairy cattle and produce cheese. Their schools are the best. Tourists are invited to Volunteer working on the farms. Once again, an example of Pura Vida, "the Pura life."

Footnote- SJO. Translate to San Jose International Airport, or Juan Santamaria Airport. It is the International Airport San Jose. Juan Santamaria was a national hero. He was killed while combating William Walkers attempt to take over the government in 1856. It is a day of parades and celebration. The second international airport is in Liberia in the Northwest near the Pacific Ocean.

Chapter 3

San Jose A city guide

"There are no foreign lands. It is the
traveler only who is foreign."
-Robert Louis Stevenson

San Jose Most people do not consider San Jose as
their number one destination. They arrive at the SJO
international airport and prefer to leave the city soon.
They want to visit the beach, or mountains quickly. But
I disagree. I prefer a couple of days in San Jose before
going elsewhere. San Jose is a beautiful colonial city
with much to offer. It is a chance to meet and greet the
local people. Also, to try the local food and drinks.
Maybe to buy some souvenirs. You can always store
the souvenirs at the hotel until you return. My favorite
hotel is the Balmoral in El Centro. San Jose translates
from Spanish as Saint Joseph's, the national holiday of
the day of San Jose.

Saint Joseph is the patron saint of Costa Rica. A special mass is celebrated on this day. It falls on March 19th.

What to see and do. National theater. The theater was opened in 1897 because the people needed a theater watch was world class to attract the best opera singers and actors from Europe. The locals placed a tax on the coffee and banana exports to construct the theater. It worked famous European entertainers started to appear in San Jose. They now have a world class Opera House, or theater. San Jose could now be proud. Guided tours are offered every day. Be sure to see the art mural of the workers loading the ship with bananas, and coffee for export. It is a classic, and not to be missed. You will visit the large auditorium. There is a coffee house and cafe to visit on the way out. Be sure to attend a concert to test the acoustics. They have a coffee or glass of wine in the cafe near the exit. The address is Calle 5, Ave 2 central.

The gold museum.

This is a must-see museum which displays pre -Columbian original and replica of gold artifacts. It is located El Centro San Jose next to the National Museum. Calle 5 Ave 2 central.

The Jade museum.

There is a gift shop. The museum has the largest collection of Jade in the Americas. Also, they exhibit some ceramics. It is located Calle 13, Ave central.

National Museum

This museum is in the former army barracks When Costa Rica had a military. Now it is a history and anthropology museum opened in 1948. It is located Calle 15, Ave 2 central.

La Sabana Metropolitan park

A very nice greenspace in the heart of San Jose. A place to get away and relax. It has a Lake, plus jogging trails, and a soccer field. The park has a large swimming pool.

Cathedral Metropolitan

Founded in 1871. Magnificent interior and windows. Escazu

An upscale neighborhood located just West of San Jose El Centro. You will find a modern shopping center, an upscale bar, a restaurant. Costa Rica craft brewing is located here. The little theater group is located here, and the Eugene O'Neill theater. Check the Tico Times newspaper for dates and times. Hotels located here are upscale as well. The hotel intercontinental is one of the most expensive in San Jose. Telephone +506-2208-2100. Next to plaza mall. Beautiful botanical grounds to walk about. Rooms expensive 240 USD.

Butterfly garden Located in barrio Amon. Enclosure has a variety of butterfly species including the blue morpho. Great warm up visit for Monte Verde.

University of Costa Rica. (UCR) UCR Was founded in 1940, an is in the east of San Jose in San Pedro. UCR Is the home of the theater Universitario. They offer a wide variety of theater arts productions. It is a part of the Fine Arts Department. (Page 136 in Molina). Check the Tico times for the schedule of plays. In San Pedro you will find the mall San Pedro. This is a four-story complex. It has a food court, cinema, a video arcade. San Pedro, the home of UCR, has numerous college bars and cafes. Mora Books. Great source of used books. English and Spanish. Calle 5, Ave 5 and 7. Mercado Central. The main market in San Jose. Always busy. They sell A to Z, Coffee to T-shirts. You name it. A shopper's delight. Located on Ave 1 central and Calle 6 and 8. It beats the supermarkets if you want variety in fresh foods.

Why visit San Jose?

The traffic can be hectic, and the city can be crowded, during peak hours. But I think it can be a pleasant surprise and well worth a visit on your way from the SJO airport to the beach, or the mountains. The Central Valley can be cool versus the hot and humid rainforest of the beach. It is a rich colonial city with excellent historic landmarks. Also, the bars and restaurants are international. There is no lack of entertainment. It is a cultural capital with music, theater, University, sports, museums, day trips, and shopping. You will not be bored my friend. It is one of my favorite cities. Viva San Jose!

Chapter 4

Hotels & Hostels in San Jose Where to sleep?

"When you travel, remember that a foreign country is not designed to make you comfortable. It's designed to make its own people comfortable."
-Clifton Fadiman

Hotels, hostels, and where to sleep?

You have many options of where to sleep in San Jose. I try to offer you options which range from budget hotels, to mid-range, end to the expensive. You can select the price range which fits you best. My favorite search engine for selecting a hotel is either booking. com, or trivago. My favorite hotel in San Jose is the Balmoral Hotel, Avenida central, between 7 and 9 streets, San Jose, Costa Rica. PO 3344-1000. Toll free 1-800-691-4865 or 506-2222-5022 email www.

balmoral.co.cr, reservations balmoral.co.cr. The hotel is newly renovated. It has the best location in San Jose El Centro. Avenida Central on El Centro. There is a free breakfast buffet and free Wi-Fi. A free gym and parking. Walking distance to historic sites and shopping. About 20 USD from airport (SJO). The Balmoral price range is moderate, 74 USD per single room. It is affordable to most travelers. The location is excellent. Bar and restaurant. Music entertainment and very cordial staff. Travel desk. Shopping on the bottom level. Large clean rooms. AC and TV. Wi-Fi, parking garage.

Across the street is the El Presidente Hotel. Across from the Balmoral in El Centro and 7th street. A standard room is 90USD. Free Wi-Fi and breakfast, tv, mini fridge. El Presidente is centrally located and spotless clean. Recently renovated. Barlan restaurant. Next to the pedestrian St and the gold museum. www. hotel-presidente.com PO BOX 2922-1000. San Jose CR. Telephone 506-2010-000. info@hotel-presidente.com.

Hotel Fleur de Lys

A Victorian house converted into an enchanting hotel. This hotel is a small hotel located in the cultural district. Native artwork can be seen on the walls of the 31 individually decorated rooms. There is a charming atrium garden with lush tropical plants. Address is Calle 13 at Avenidas. Telephone 500-2223-1200. The rooms have a moderate price of 51USD. It is a short walk to the

National Theatre. Near the city center. Clean with good housekeeping. reservaciones@hotelfleurdelys.com.

Gran Hotel

Jimmy Carter has stayed there. I once occupied the John Wayne suite. Rooms are a bargain. They are priced at 50USD. A great breakfast on the top floor overlooking the city. There is a popular piano bar on the patio. They also serve coffee. It is great for people watching and seeing the passing parade. It is a good value and has a friendly staff. Casino in the basement. Travel desk. Even if you don't stay at the Gran just walk through the hotel to get a feel for the history. Gran Hotel Calle 3 between Central Ave. and Ave 2 El Centro. This hotel has a historical charm about it since it is in a historic building. Built in 1930. 107 rooms. Near Gold museum and National theater are next door.

Hotel Grano de Oro

Near El centro on Calle 30 between Aves 2 and 4. A boutique hotel on the expensive side of the budget. Standard room 150USD. Deluxe room 234USD. Family friendly. 40 rooms. Free parking and wi-fi and gourmet restaurant. TV and AC. Surcharge for breakfast. Located in a renovated old Victorian home in a residential district east of El Centro San Jose www.hotelgandeoro. Telephone 506-2255-3322. Expensive price range.

Hostel Bekuo

This is a hotel for budget travel. Address 325 Meters Oeste soon Los Yoses San Jose 2050. Telephone +506 2234-1091. Great location close to restaurants and shops. Good price. Dorm 13 USD and room 32USD. Clean and nice basic rooms.

Costa Rica Backpackers Hostel

Located Ave 6 Calle 21-25. Great location and friendly staff near El Centro San Jose. Near bars and restaurants. Kitchen facilities and free internet. Dorm rooms 12USD. Private rooms 35USD. Laundry and security lockers. Outdoor terrace and swimming pool. Game room. No curfew. Near the train station. Happy hour every day.

Hotel Costa Rica Morazán

Close to El Centro. Hotel, Casino, and walk to Gold museum. Includes breakfast. Free wi-fi. Adjacent to Morazán park. Restaurant and bar. TV and AC. Standard room 47USD. Telephone +506 2222-4722. Location 1st Ave and 7th street. hmorazanar@gmail.com.

Costa Rica Marriott San Jose

For those who prefer luxury book the Costa Rica Marriott San Jose. Rates range from 239USD to 319USD, or 1,000USD. Rewards members pay 171USD.

Some rooms have a mountain view. The hotel borders on a coffee plantation. Address is 700 Meters from Bridgestone/Firestone La Ribesa de Belen, Heredia providence, Heredia, Costa Rica. Not far from the airport. Telephone +506 2298 0000.

Hacienda Alta Gracia in Santa Elena San Jose

This is a five-star resort. It is very close and popular with couples and gets a 9.4 rating by its guests. A deluxe luxury suite is 391USD. It has its own private landing stripe and is served by Sansa Air, a popular small airline. The hacienda, or ranch, was constructed to blend in with nature. It has a pool, horseback riding, and biking. It is a blend of luxury with nature. Telephone +506 2105-3000 or toll free 1-855-969-1054.

The money in Costa Rice is the CRC, or colon. Currently the exchange rate is 590 colons equals one USD. Google Oanda.com to stay up to date on the exchange rate and download a free cheat sheet. In summary, San Jose and vicinity has an abundance of hotels at various levels, styles, and ranges from the one-star hostels, to the mid-level, up to five-star haciendas. You can find the hotel that best meets your needs.

Airport Hotels for SJO

Some travelers prefer to stay near the SJO airport for convenience. There are numerous hotels near the airport, and some offer free shuttles period but remember, there are numerous activities to keep you busy in El Centro San Jose. However, you can hit the ground running early in the morning if you are traveling out of SJO airport.

Holiday Inn Express Airport San Jose room rate is 106 USD. Located 1km East of the Airport. Alajuela San Jose 2-1017 www.holidayinnexpress/hotels/us/en/reservation.com Telephone 1-888-890-0224 or 1-888-233-9450. This Hotel gets an excellent rating of 4.4 of 5. Includes breakfast, free parking, and free Internet. Swimming pool, and business center. Fitness center, and free airport shuttle.

Berlor Airport Inn Located 2km East of Airport. Free drop off shuttle. Room rates start 59USD. Rooms have TV, AC, Wi-Fi, and free breakfast. Swimming pool, restaurant and bar. Tour desk. Volcano 45minute drive.

Juan Santamaria International Airport (SJO) Alajuela, San Jose. Next to the Pan American Highway. Free airport shuttle. Rooms have AC, TV and Wi-Fi. Free parking. A daily breakfast buffet with tropical fruits. Tour desk. The rooms are surrounded by trees and a garden.

Swimming pool. Room rates start at 63 USD.

Chapter 5

Restaurants and Cafes in San Jose

"If you reject the food, ignore the customs,
fear the religion and avoid the people,
you might as well stay home."
-James A. Michener

San Jose Restaurants and where to eat. The comida tipica, cosada or typical food in Costa Rica which is basically rice and beans. Pollo (chicken), bistec (steak), and pescado (fish) are popular. San Jose offers a variety of restaurants. A tourist can save money at lunch by ordering a set menu of the daily items usually composed of rice, beans, meat and a salad. Of course, pescado (fish) is popular from the Pacific, and the Caribbean. Platanos Maduros, or ripe plantains, grilled with brown sugar is also popular. The choices are almost endless. San Jose restaurants, cafes, or Soda. San Jose is very international when it comes to restaurants, almost like NYC, but orientated toward Latin America, and Spanish. You will find A to Z food in San Jose restaurants. They range the spectrum from small soda cafes, to Latin, Central America, Vietnamese, Fusion, Vegetarian, South American, Norte Americano, Italian and Seafood. It is your choice. There is also McDonalds, Burger King, and Kentucky Fried Chicken. My favorite over the years is Chille's. It is open 24 hours. Chille's is a soda café and bar. Popular with the local Ticos. It is on Ave Central down the street from the Balmoral hotel, Where I usually stay. It makes a late end of the night stop. Located Ave Central and Calle up from the city bus station. Drinks and coffee all night. Chille's is an institution in San Jose. It has been there for over 100 years.

What is a soda cafe in Costa Rica? A soda is unique. They differ from Norte Americano. Like Chille's they usually are open 24 hours. It is a diner 24-hour cafe with food and alcohol. They are like your local corner restaurant. Chille's Is a good place to people watch. I call it watching the "passing parade" of people. While having a glass of wine, a beer, or cafe. The waitresses are very attentive and helpful. The crowd is a mixture of locals, and international. The typical food is the cosadas or chicken, beef, fish, or pork chops with rice, corn and peas. Followed by a cold beer.

The Balmoral has a good Restaurant, and music for the evening. Music on the second floor with a nice view of the street. El Patio del Balmoral is the restaurant. Located on the ground floor of El Balmoral at Ave

Central Calle 7 and 9. Telephone +506-2222-5022. It is a combination bar and restaurant. Prices are moderate. Service is good. Drinks are large.

Cafe Mundo A popular Italian café Located in an old historic Mansion with a large garden. They offer indoor, or outside dining. This quality restaurant is popular with locals and tourists. The café features pasta and pizza, which makes it popular with families, kids and teens. Moderate prices. Located Calle 15 and Ave 9 in North Central San Jose not far from the Hotel Rincon.

La Esquina de Buenos Argentine steaks house restaurant. Good value. A mixed grille cuts of steak. Cozy atmosphere, Spanish tile floor. Great wine list. Candle lit tables. On the menu are cosada, pasta, mixed grille, and lava cakes for dessert. Great choice for steak lovers. You can't go wrong. You will think you are in South America. Located Calle 11 Ave near the Colonial hotel. Telephone +506-2223-1909.

Tin Jo Restaurant Popular Chinese, or Asian fusion menu for those who want a change from rice and beans. Vegetarian menu selections. People like the Hung Pao shrimp. Not expensive. Quality and service good. Address Calle 11 between Ave 8 and 11. Telephone +506-2221-7605.

Grano de oro Restaurant. This is a popular upscale restaurant. Lunch and dinner. Specialty is a fusion menu using Costa Rican and European foods. Costa Rica cuisine. The dining experience is formal. The menu includes these popular selections, sea bass, eggs benedict, duck and lamb shank. Great dining experience if you like the formal presentation. Great wine list. Somewhat on the expensive side, but quality. Located in Grano de oro hotel San Jose in a Victoria type home Calle 30. Telephone +506-2255-3322.

Mariscos Poseidon. Great for seafood. Mariscos is a seafood soup, my favorite. Not expensive. Just add rice to the soup. It is located near the central and market the banco national between Ave 1 and 3 and Calle 6.

Central Market (Mercado) located Ave 1 and 6 between Calle 6 and 8. It is a combination of a flea and street market. You can buy food to take home, or there are food stalls for dining. You will find typical food of Costa Rica such as cosada. Casada is a mixture of rice, beans, salad with either fish, beef, or chicken. A great place to eat for those on a budget. While you are at the Mercado you may want to buy a souvenir, or t-shirt. Street markets are a lot of fun. For desert try Pop's Ice cream. The best! The kids will love it.

Mama's Place. Very popular restaurant with locals, office workers, and budget travelers. Good food at a good price. Varied menu but mostly Italian. Located near the large post office building. There is a plate of the day to save some money. Address in downtown San Jose on Ave 1, El Carmen, SJCR.

Alma de café. Located in the National theater across from the Grand Hotel in Centro San Jose. Lovely European setting serving coffee and cappuccino with crepes and quiche. A nice place to stop and relax, then see the artwork.

Park Café and Antiques. Located at de las Americas at Calle 48, San Jose, CR Telephone +506-2290-6324. The North East corner of Sabana park. The café and shop are in an historic hacienda home, with a courtyard. The antiques are for sale. The menu is a Fusion of European and international foods. The chief chef is Richard who has studied in worked in Europe. His partner in the cafe is Louise France. Many reviewers have called the cafe the "best in Costa Rica." Others have called the cafe "foods for the gods."

Another favorite of mine for the budget traveler is the bar and restaurant La Embajada. Ave 1 at Calle Central. It is also a sports bar with TV's constantly showing soccer, or football. it also has a jukebox. Beer and rum drinks are cheap. Food plates are also cheap. Locals love this place. They flock here to Meet their friends, drink the El presidente cerveza, and watch football. They Open at 10:00 AM and close at midnight. They serve the Costa Rican drink called "Guaro." It is a cheap rum made locally like the white lighting in the USA. The most popular name brand rum is the Centenario in Costa Rica for international sales.

This book should help you book your travel destination and find the best airline reservation. My goal is to inspire you to travel. To follow your dreams. The promise is that you do not have to be rich to make your travel dreams come true. Just be flexible in your planning and be willing to sacrifice to follow a budget. The waterfalls, and beaches can be yours. Costa Rica is a tropical adventure and just waiting for you.

Chapter 6

Bars and Pubs in San Jose

"The pub, like all over the world, was a place for debate and discussion, but the exchange of views and opinions, but argument and for the working out of problems. It was a forum, a parliament, a fountain of wisdom and a cesspool of nonsense."
-Alex La Guma (A walk in the night and other stories.)
Hoxton pub. Located at the Barrio exchange.
Ave 11 San Pedro. www.hoxloncr.com

This pub is owned by two British expats. They serve bars and English pub food such as fish and chips. Food is reasonable from 8-16 USD. Hoxton is a popular nighttime hangout for the young local crowd, girl's night out is on Tuesday. There is a live DJ and usually crowded. Located in an old mansion. Cheap drinks and dancing.

Jazz Club San Pedro. Great place for concerts and live bands. A different band every night. A mix of local and international bands and musicians. Located 150 meters North of Toyota, Paseo Colon, San Pedro on the Eastern outskirts of San Jose near the University of Costa Rica. Popular with the tourist and locals. They have a branch Jazz club in Escaza. There is a cover charge.

Club Vertigo. It is known for the DJ's and dancing. Great all for night clubbing. Located near colonel Centro, San Jose, CR Telephone +506-2257-8424.

Chille's Sports Bar and Grill. San Pedro El Centro San Pedro Telephone +506-2271-2334 www.chillessports.com popular with locals and expats. Burgers and wings. Flat screen TV's. Variety of sports. Pop and top 40 music. Sports from CR, USA and UK.

El Patio Bar and Restaurant in the Balmoral Hotel. The upstairs bar is popular serving numerous beers, rum and wine. They feature live music on Wednesday through Friday's. Located on central Ave with views of the passing parade of people. An Oasis in the center of the city. Food is fresh. Seafood, salads, and pizza. Local dishes with rice and beans. Great food in a great location. Chille's. café and bar. Located central Ave at Calle 9, El Centro. Near the Balmoral. Chille's is a favorite of mine. Open 24 hours. Favorite of locals (Ticos) and tourist. Great for people watching. Good budget class café and bar. Bar has a full range from beer, wine, rum, and various mix drinks. The Costa

Rican menu comma and breakfast. Great for after a night of partying.

Bar Morzan. Calle 7 between Ave 1 and Ave 3 Typical local bar period not expensive. Beer, wine, and mixed drinks. Multiple TV's for sports. Sports betting window.

Public house Irish pub. 150 meters North of Toyota, Paseo Colon, San Jose. +506-8432-7991. Popular with locals and expats. Variety of craft beers. Multiple TV's for sports fans. Excellent pub grub food. Not expensive. Best beer of Costa Rica is Imperial, or Pilsen. The best rum is centenarian.

Bar and cafe Embajada. Avenida 1 and Calle 1. Sports bar with mini TV's. Football all day long. Serves many Imperial and Pilsen beers, cheap. Local rum also popular. Many local people with a few tourists period very good local food Platters such as steak polo or fish grilled with rice and beans. This bar is one of my favorites in San Jose. A good place to meet locals an experience the culture. Good food, good beer, at a reasonable price near El Centro. The Embajada serves a local drink called "guaro," a Sugar cane liquor, or homemade rum. it is served as a shop, very strong, and cheap alcohol drink.

Castro's Bar and Discotheque. Great for dancing. Old-fashioned Latin disco with salsa and reggae. Located North of Avenue 1 El Centro between Calle 22 and Calle 20. Near Ave 11 There are 3 levels of wooden dance floors. Popular with both older and younger singles. Telephone +506-2256-8789.

Miraflores Disco Club. Popular place to dance and party. Open only on the weekends. Located in Hacienda on the outskirts of San Jose.

As you can see San Jose is a great restaurant, and partytown. There is something for everyone's lifestyle. When you get to the jungle you will not have a variety of things to do. San Jose is a good city stop in the arrival of Costa Rica, in the departing.

Domestic Airlines It is easy and fast to travel on the domestic airlines of Costa Rica. The 2 popular domestic airlines are Nature Air and Sansa. They fly from San Jose, and Liberia. Some of these small planes can land on the beaches such as Corcovado and Tortuguero. They serve Arenal and Monteverde as well. Operations at nature air have temporarily halted because of a deadly crash two years ago. They are waiting on a crash investigation finding. Nature flies mainly the Otter Turbo prop produced in Canada and the newer Cessna caravan turbo prop from the USA.

Sansa is operating. They primarily use the Cessna caravan, and they have ordered the new model of the caravan.

It's five o'clock somewhere."
-Jimmy Buffett and Alan Jackson

Chapter 7

Day Trips from San Jose

"For my part, I travel not to go anywhere, but to go. I travel for travel's sake. The great affair is to move."
-Robert Louis Stevenson

Day tours from San Jose. Some tourist have limited time to explore outside San Jose, and there are those who prefer to keep their hotel rooms. San Jose, because of its central location, makes it easy to take day tours either by a travel agency, or renting a car. Also, there are local Nature Air, in Sansa Air for transportation. After a city tour you may take a coffee farm tour (Such as Brit coffee), visit.

Coffee tour cafe Britt. A two-hour tour where the guide explains every step of harvesting and roasting the coffee beans to the finished product. Includes coffee tasting and shopping period cost is 20 USD with a pickup at the hotel.

LaSelva Rainforest outside San Jose, a rafting tour on the Rio Pacure and Poas volcano National Park, or a canopy tour. Tours can be Arranged at your hotel desk. Expediciones Tropicales, Costa Rica, or Costa Rica Expeditions can make the arrangement. De Safio Costa Rica Tours La Fortuna can also book trips for you. Contact De Safio at 1-800-818-0020 or in CR at +506-2479-0020. Don't forget about bird watching tours. Costa Rica is a prime country for bird watching. There are some 900 bird species. Perhaps you will see McCaw parrots, Hummingbirds, or the Toucan with a huge bill or beak. The Quetzal (the national bird) Is colorful but shy and hard to see. My favorite is the Toucan which flew over my patio every morning in Manuel Antonio. Mounteverde is another prime place to see birds. Expediciones Tropicales, and Essential Costa Rica offers a unique day trip which they call rainforest adventure, or 3 in 1 adventure. This includes a canopy tour, River tour, and walking bridge between tall trees. A great full day adventure. The best way to experience Costa Rica is by visiting its national parks if you have a week or more. Most tourists want to see the beaches, waterfall, volcanoes, a canopy tour, and rafting. Everyone comes to see the wildlife.

Poas Volcano National park. The poas volcano is located a one-hour drive from San Jose to Alaquela. Try to see the volcano crater before the clouds move in is best to go in the morning. After going through the entrance gate, you go to the top to see the crater. The view is exciting, especially if you have never seen one before. The elevation is 8800 feet. Be sure to take a jacket. The Poas volcano is considered active, and sometimes the Rangers limit the entrance of tourists when there is an eruption. You are free to hike around the crater if there is no eruption. The entrance fee is 19 USD at the gate. You can also buy the ticket online to save time and worry. It is the perfect day trip if you want to keep your hotel room in San Jose.

Ziplining one day trip from San Jose. This tour can be made with Go Tours Costa Rica. It is the best zip line tour in the Central Valley where San Jose is located. They have 12 zip lines with experienced guides. The trip is 73 USD. They supply hotel pick up and drop off. They have numerous other trips available. Lunch is provided. Contact Go Tours Costa Rica in the USA 770-206-8019, or in CR at +506-4030-1417. Email travel@ gotourscostarica.com. If the person is too large for the zip line you can instead go for a guided nature walk or visit the butterfly farm in Hummingbird gardens. La Paz Waterfalls and gardens. Butterflies, and hummingbirds. This is a great place for nature lovers to visit on a one-day trip from San Jose. The waterfalls are spectacular. Be prepared to walk the extensive hiking trails. The garden of La Paz is located on the slopes of the Poas volcano, about One hour from San Jose. The largest volcano is called In Spanish, La Catorata de la Paz, or the peace waterfall. It is rich in biodiversity. An extra added attraction is a butterfly garden, a Hummingbird garden which you encounter as you hike the trail. There are viewing platforms along the trail. You can spend as much as 3 hours touring the la Paz gardens and waterfall. There are 5 waterfalls. Enjoy the beautiful plants, Especially the orchids. A must see during your trip to Costa Rica. The entrance fee is paid at the gate. The fee for an adult is 42 USD. That includes the waterfall, the poas park with entrance to the butterfly and Hummingbird gardens. There is a visitor center, a shop, and a small museum. Poas National Park was the first in all of Costa Rica and is the most popular since it is new San Jose. It is best to visit during the week when the locals are at work. Try to arrive early in the morning. How to travel to Poas National Park. The best over land route from San Jose is to take Hwy 120 N 2 Vara Blanca. Continue to Poas. At the entrance gate pay a fee of 42 USD this fee allows you to visit the volcano, the waterfalls, and the gardens. Inside you will find the peace lodge, and the restaurant. You can travel by auto or bus. Don't forget sunscreen, hat, walking shoes, Camera, water comma and light jacket. The Poas waterfalls and gardens are a must see for nature lovers. This is why you travel to Costa Rica. Pura Vida!

Sarapiqui one day rafting tour from San Jose. You should depart your hotel, either driving or by a tour group, at 6:30 AM. It will be a long day. The ride takes you the Sarapiqui Valley, which was known in the 1880s as an important location for the United fruit company. As bananas gave way in importance the Sarapiqui river became important for tourism. The River is popular for white water rafting. As the River meanders South toward the Caribbean It passes by the popular Selva

Verde eco lodge. Along the way you will mostly see sloths, monkeys, toucans, frogs, possibly snakes. There is beautiful scenery along the banks. The Sarapiqui is as a class 3 rapids, which is excellent for families and kids under 12 years of age. Group or single escorted tours to Poas, or La Paz Waterfalls can be booked with travel agencies. Options are Costa Rica experts, Telephone 1-866-321-1557, or costaricaexperts.com. Also, you can use trip advisors go to tripadvisors.com. One more is Viator tours prices range from 104USD to 137USD hotel pick up and return or, use Google, or the hotel tour desk. Costa Rica is one of the best places to view wildlife. Of course, Africa is also popular. But Costa Rica is unique for its biodiversity, it's rain forests and cloud forests.

Selva Verde Lodge. It is accessible by a day trip, or overnight drive from San Jose. It is a rainforest reserve in the heart of Sarapiqui. The lodge is built next to the Sarapiqui river with great views. It is a 2-hour drive from San Jose, and the dirt road at the end is not well maintained. You can rent a car or book with a travel agency. The lodge has 41 rooms, a magnificent pool and spa. A standard room is 109 USD. Day trips are popular. Contact the lodge from the USA at 1-855-516-1092. Or CR +506-2761-1800. Great location. Restaurant and bar. Gift shop, Wi-Fi A nice getaway from the city to enjoy the real rainforest. Day tour bird watching. Costa Rica is a prime country for bird watching. Each year birds migrate here from the North, mostly in December to February. What they call the "dry season" when the trails are not too muddy. Over 300 native bird species make their home in Costa Rica. You perhaps will see MaCaw parrots, hummingbirds, there is the scarlet McCaw, green MaCaw (which can go for 5000USD on the illegal market.)

Birdwatching. Costa Rica is the ideal place for the serious birder. Costa Rica has an array of birds, exotic and rare. They are colorful as well. The scarlet Macaw and the brilliant Quetzal are good examples. It is a birder's paradise. Costa Rica has over 900 species of birds which equals 10% of the world bird population. The Toucan is My favorite. La Selva Is the ideal place to see as many Birds as possible. It is the home of the famous research station. Rainforest adventures located in Limon Offers a birders tour, in Atlantic park reserve. They can arrange for your transfer From San Jose. Includes breakfast, lunch, and guide. Includes all entrance fees. RT Ride on the bus or coach.

Spirogyra Butterfly garden. Located in San Jose. A virtual Oasis in the city. Located near the 200 highway. Just a taxi ride from your hotel in El Centro. An impressive number of butterflies for viewing. Located in barrio Amon. Entrance fee 7 USD telephone +506-222-2937. Includes the famous morpho. Beautiful gardens.

Chapter 8

Manuel Antonio The beach and National park

"Twenty years from now you will be more disappointed by the things you didn't do them by the ones you did do. So, throw off the bowlines, sail away from the safe harbor. Catch the trade winds in your sails. Explore. Dream. Discover."
-Mark Twain

A barrel full of monkeys. I enjoyed my trip to Manuel Antonio. My hotel was next to the park. Each morning I would sit on my patio and watch a daily parade of squirrel monkeys leave their tree and go in a line to the park. They would stop where a chef gave them the leftover slices of fruit and bananas. They would have a heaping good time. It was entertainment. I called it a "barrel full of monkeys."

Capuchin monkey. Most often called the white-faced capuchin. There are 4 species of monkeys in Costa Rica. Tourists are most interested in the "white faced." The squirrel monkey is a smaller mammal found mostly in Manuel Antonio, where the white faced is found mostly in Arenal and Monte Verde. The howler monkey is known for its loud vocal "howl" mostly at nighttime. The "howl" Comes from the male in the rainforest. Perhaps he is lonely or is establishing his dominance of the territory. Day trip from San Jose gives the tourists a taste of the biodiversity of Costa Rica. Now it's time to venture out into the national parks my first stop is my favorite, Manuel Antonio. It is also the most popular with tourists. A major reason for the tourists is the spectacular beaches. The rainforest is another reason. There are many species of monkeys. It is the perfect tropical paradise! And don't forget the sloth and Toucans. There is a total of 27 national parks in Costa Rica. The management of the parks is under the central control and decision making of the ministry of environmental Protection and sustainable tourism. My favorite part to visit is Manuel Antonio National Park on the central Pacific. Manuel Antonio has always been my favorite. It has a beautiful park with hiking trails. You can see wildlife such as monkeys and sloth in their natural environment. See the flora and fauna of the rainforest. Listen to the monkey's howls at night. Relax on the beach and watch the passing parade of tourists. Life is Pura Vida!

Things to do in Manuel Antonio National Park. the park is known for its rich diversity in plants and animals. The park is small, and the hiker can easily walk it in a day. You will be required at the gate entrance to have a certified guide, Or an official Ranger. The gate entry fee is currently 15USD. For your visit be sure to have binoculars. Your guide will have binoculars just in case. Bring your Camera and a sun hat. Also, sunscreen. You will need a swimsuit, of course a bottle of water. It is closed on Mondays. Wildlife is diverse. You will see various breeds of monkey's, sloths, iguanas and hundreds of bird species. It is the best place for birding. The trails are well marked and do not have difficult inclines. It is best to go in the mornings. Walking tours taken with a guide can cost 59 USD. Do not bring snacks into the park. Monkeys might try to raid your backpack for food. The gate closes at 4:00 PM. At the gate they will give you a map. The trails are well marked with wooden signs. You will always know where you are in the park. Efrain's Nature tours, with an office near the gate, is another way to book a tour with a guide. Telephone +506-2777-9356 Typical cost is 59-79USD.

Other tour groups are Costa Rica experts, or Manuel tours or, go to your hotel desk.

There are many activities to experience outside the park. For example, relax on Manuel

Antonio beach. Or Espadilla Sur beach. Zip lines to get the adrenaline flowing, try ziplining. The popularity of zip lining grows every day, kids as well as adults. Enjoy the excitement and adventure of connecting to the cable and sliding over the rainforest. Want to try? Sign up with Manuel Antonio zipline adventures. Telephone +506-6218-1036. This company has "Top of the line" safety equipment. 75USD. The Home Office is in Narango, 35-minute drive from Manuel Antonio. They can pick you up at your hotel.

Need more adventure? Now it is time to try a 4-wheel drive ATV. There are several ATV tour groups. Off-road manual Antonio is a good one to do your booking. They will pick you up at your hotel. Be warned, you will get muddy! Horseback tours are available. Manuel Antonio park is the most popular, to visit. People like the biodiversity which is located in a small area for hiking. The climate is appealing with both dry and wet rain forests. The beaches and oceans are appealing. The Walking trails are easy. There is an abundance of monkeys, including the howlers. Everybody loves the adorable docile sloths. It is often called "the jewel" of Costa Rica.

Dominical. This is a rustic beach town home to surfers and backpackers. It is a 30-minute drive from Manuel Antonio. It can be reached by bus, rental car, or Sansa and Nature Air from San Jose. There are ample budget class hotels or hostels. By Hwy you take 243 to wear it intersects Hwy 34 S. The airport is in Quepos. Besides surfing there is the Poza Azul waterfall. Also, see Hacienda Baru, a wildlife refuge. The Baru has many bird species in reptiles. To book a surfing adventure contact Dominical Surf Adventure Telephone +506-8897-9540. They also book rafting trips.

Hacienda Baru lodge, is a series of cabins near the Baru beach. 96 USD with entrance to the Baru refugee reserve. La Parcola Restaurant in Dominical. Budget class 12 USD. Panoramic ocean views. Excellent pizza. Located at the Costa Paraiso Hostel. Iguana tours Quepos Inn Manuel Antonio. They offer a variety of tours ranging from rafting, horseback riding, 2 zip line. It is a reputable to tour company on the central Pacific, telephone +506-2777-2062.

Sportfishing in Costa Rica. The dedicated sportfishing tourist flocks to the Pacific Ocean of Costa Rica. The waters here are world class sportfishing. Sailfish and the Marlin is the goal. December to April is the prime time for hooking a sailfish. You can book your trip at Marina Perez Quepos. It can be expensive. Nicoya Peninsula is another option for sports fishing. You could catch tuna or dorado or bill fish. Most people practice "catch and release," most keep their prize Marlin. To place on the wall at home.

Chapter 9

Hotels and Hostels in Manuel Antonio and Quepos

"Home is where the heart is, and my
heart is where I am at the moment."
-Lily Leung

Hotel Costa Verde. Located at a turn off the popular and busy beach road from Quepos to the center of Manuel Antonio and Hwy 518. Be careful because the road is in a hilly area and very narrow. It is called the Manual Antonio road, Quepos Manuel Antonio. This road is about 5 miles travel distance from Quepos to Antonio. When you see the El Avion Located by a C122 Fairchild aircraft then you are there. Inside the grounds, they have a 727 jet. Turn off the road into the jungle driveway. The office is up front to check you into your rooms. The rooms are scattered about a Bluff overlooking the Pacific. A luxury room is built into a restored 727 jet aircraft. The average is 147 USD. The rooms are spacious and have a fantastic panoramic view of the ocean. The room has a small kitchen, and a patio on the back to listen to the sounds of the rainforest and observe monkeys and birds. The large pool is a short walk down the Hill near the beach. The hotel has a restaurant, bar and lounge, Wi-Fi and free parking. The rooms have AC, and cable TV. A stay at the Costa Verde is a real treat. I would return. Contact reservations@ costaverde.com Telephone 1-800-854-7965.

Hotel La Mariposa. Expensive category. The turn off from Quepos road is before you reach Manuel Antonio near the Manuel Antonio nature park and wildlife refuge. The hotel is known for its beautiful well designed and maintained gardens and grounds. There are 50 rooms. The view of the ocean is superb. The wooden furniture is carefully hand made. The typical price for a room is 240 USD. Telephone 1-800-572-6440. www.lamariposa.com.

Hotel Villabosque. Near the main entrance to Manuel Antonio National Park. Telephone +506-2777-0463. Price 100 USD. Pool, AC, LCD TV and Wi-Fi. Excellent bar and restaurant. Located 3 minutes walking distance from the park to Espadilla beach. Turn off Quepos highway at Marlin restaurant. Rooms are Immaculate. Great location and quality.

Torino Backpackers beach hostel. 17 USD. It is the bed in a dormitory style. It is close to the beach an easy walk to town, bus stop, and to the Antonio park. Telephone +506-4701-2735. Wi-Fi free, room for TV, there is a patio and balcony. Free parking share kitchen. Comfy beds. Grocery store nearby. Restaurants and bars in town.

Hotel Manuel Antonio by the National Park. Puntarenas, Manuel Antonio 60601 Costa Rica. 5-minute walk to beach and 3-minute walk to Manuel Antonio National Park. Pool, garden, sitting porch. Tour desk, restaurant serves as a bar. Wi-Fi, parking, AC. Quepos ten-minute drive. Great location. My favorite for location and value. I enjoyed sitting on the porch where I would watch monkeys one by one start to move from there sleeping place on the edge of the village into the rainforest. What a free sideshow! A barrel full of monkeys! We must not lose them! Be careful when standing under a tree full of monkeys. They like to throw their "feces" onto the watching tourists.

Wide mouth Frog Backpackers. This is a budget class hostel. Shared bathrooms, kitchenette. Shared dining area. Shared double dorm rooms. There are some private rooms. Price 12 USD. You will have to take the bus to Manuel Antonio for the park or beach.

Mellenium Hostel.

30 USD. Manuel Antonio. Telephone +506-4700-2631 Next to National Park. Views of the park. Guests use a common kitchen, cable TV, wi-fi. Private bathroom. Bar, AC. Pool and garden for relaxation. Clean and spacious. Take 518 road and exit hostel on road turn off. Close to park.

Best Western hotel Kamuk and casino. Located in Quepos, A small fishing village on the Pacific. It was named for the Quepos indigenous Indians. It is the gateway to manual Antonio National Park. The hotel is located across the road from the beach and near the Marina Pez Vela. The sailboat tours and fishing boats depart from the Marina. The rooms at the Best Western are 80 USD. This includes breakfast, pool, AC and TV. The rooms include modern features. Telephone +506-2777-0379. There is a restaurant at the top floor with a panoramic view of the Pacific. The downtown location is near shopping and supermarkets. It is easy from Quepos to take the city bus or taxi to Manuel Antonio and the beach.

Gaia hotel and Reserve. This hotel is surrounded by the jungle or reserve. It is classified as a five-star, all-inclusive hotel for adults and nonsmoking only. It is located about halfway between Quepos and Manuel Antonio. There are 20 rooms. Near El Cerro on the Quepos highway 618. This is a boutique hotel 259 USD for a standard King size bed. Free shuttle to the beach. This hotel is my selection for a pricey hotel. Gaia reservations. Telephone 1-800-226-2515 or reservations@gaiahr.com.

Coco Beach Hotel Manuel Antonio. The location and view of the ocean is the outstanding feature. The price is 57 USD. Great views of the sunset. It is located adjacent to the Karahe Hotel. Punta arenas 60601CR. Telephone +506-2777-0165. Free Wi-Fi, pool, with beautiful grounds. You can see monkeys in the mornings. Offers "humble furnished rooms." Needs a refurbish. Great view is from the balcony.

As you can see, Manuel Antonio has a variety of places to eat and sleep. The prices range from budget, to moderate, and pricey. The backpack traveler will have many to choose from as well as the tourist with a large wallet. Tours are abundant to choose from and there are options for the independent hiker. Biodiversity is the key term to remember, especially in Manuel Antonio park, you will see Toucans, Colorful parrots, sloth, squirrel monkeys, white faced monkeys, howler monkeys and iguanas. This is why Manuel Antonio park is so popular with the tourists because of the biodiversity.

Chapter 10

Restaurants and Cafes in Manuel Antonio

"Travel is like a great blank canvas, and the painting on the canvas is only limited by one's imagination."
-Ross Morley

You will find places to eat all along the road from Quepos to the beach and park the at Manuel Antonio. You have many choices. My favorite in central Manuel Antonio is Marlins. This is a popular outdoor dining place for seafood and tropical drinks. Across from the beach and a short walk to the park. Prices to moderate. Service and food are excellent. Also great for people watching.

El Avion Restaurant and Bar. Located on the Quepos connector highway Directly across from Costa Verde hotel. Great panoramic view overlooking the ocean. When you see the retired aircraft Fairchild 123 you are there. They use the fuselodge of the plane as a bar. It is a must see and be seen restaurant. Enjoy the sunsets over the Pacific while sipping your favorite tropical cocktail, or glass of wine. El Avion Is considered to be priced moderate to expensive. No doubt about it, El Avion is a quality restaurant. El Avion is popular with seafood lovers. They offer a variety from the menu. Examples are calamari, shrimp, yellowfin tuna steaks, and the famous grilled fish of the day. For steak eaters there is the NY Angus beef. For small appetizers there are tacos, hamburger, and shrimp with rice. El Avion Has one bar on each floor. Drinks range from cold domestic beers, imported beers, wines, and mixed drinks such as margaritas and daiquiris. Salud amigos y amigas!

The Hawg and Bill Bar and Restaurant. Frente playa Manuel Antonio. Telephone +506-2777-3211. Across from the beach off the Quepos highway and the turn off to Manuel Antonio park. Also, across the street from the Marlin restaurant. Great views of the beach. Known for music and sports TV. Typical bar food with cold beer, and various mixed drinks. Two for one happy hour all day. Moderate prices. The owner is a fanatic for the famous "hawg" Harley Davidson motorcycle. He moved to Costa Rica from the USA.

Bar Jolly Roger. Located in the Byblos resort and casino. Manuel Antonio 60601. Telephone+506-2777-0411. This is a popular sports bar known for its wings and burgers. Just off the Quepos highway 618 Before arriving in Manuel Antonio. Moderate pricing.

Buru Restaurant. Located next to the entrance of Manuel Antonio park. Telephone +506-2777-3015. Buru serves typical food of Costa Rico such as cosadas. The seafood is popular. All at great prices. A definite local favorite.

Ronny's Café and Bar. This is located off the beaten path giving it an exotic feel of being lost. It is often called a "hidden gem." It sits high up on a Ridge and has beautiful views of the Pacific. Ronny, a Tico, is the owner. They specialize in fresh seafood and their banana flanke is the best! Make the turn off the main road. It is not easy to get to, but it is well worth your time. The view at sunset is stunning.

El Sol Restaurant and bar. The best view of the beach in the heart of Manuel Antonio beach. Telephone +506-2777-7003. Happy hour and beautiful sunsets. Serves steaks, lobster, and typical Costa Rican food. Come for happy hour, the sunset, and stay for dinner. Moderate to pricey menu. You have no lack of choices when it comes to food in Manuel Antonio. Prices have been increasing because Antonio has become very popular. To save money stay to specials, or appetizers. Maybe bring your own lunch and water in the park for the park.

Super Joseth Market and Liquor store. Front of playa Manuel Antonio on the Quepos highway. Telephone +506-2777-7001. Email superjoseth2@yahoo.com. This is a popular tourist mini market with beach supplies, liquor, and beer. It has everything you need for the beach (playa), or self catering in your hotel room. I liked the colorful towels with birds and animals. It is close to the Marlin restaurant.

On my Last trip I flew Nature Air round trip SJO to Quepos/Manuel Antonio. The trip was safe and without incident. The rate was 160 USD. Email reservations@ natureair.com. Telephone +506-2299-6000. Prices can vary according to seasons or availability. Telephone Sansa at 1-855-781-6703. Prices start at 40 USD one way.

In summary, Manuel Antonio is one of the Top destinations on the Pacific coast in Costa Rica. The major reason to travel here is the National Park. It is a humid rainforest environment. People come here to see the monkeys, birds, and the sloths. The beaches give you an exotic view and sunset. It is a "must see." The park is a rainforest "paradise."

Chapter 11

Sportfishing

"If I fished only to capture fish, my fishing
trips would have ended long ago."
-Zane Grey

Costa Rica is home to some of the best sportfishing and
deep-sea fishing in the Americas. Quepos is popular as
a base for charter sportfishing. Sportfishing is big here.
Start your search for a charter boat at Pez Vela marina
just south of the city center. December to April Are the
popular months, especially for sailfish. The other fish
are Marlin, dorado, tuna, wahoo, and amber jack. Many
world records have been set here. You have come to
the right place if you like sports fishing. The cost of a
typical charter boat can be expensive. It is best to share
a boat. The cost can run from 300 USD to 900 USD.
Be prepared for sticker shock! Perhaps dealing directly
with the charter boat captain can reduce the price.

Most boat captains' practice "catch and release." Some fishermen want a trophy or filet the fish for dinner. Catch and release supports the idea of eco-sustainability. Where to book your charter fishing boat? There are several options.

1. Walk the docks at Marina Pez Vela And put the word out. You will get offers.
2. Quepos sail fishing charters. Telephone +506-2777-2025. They also offer packages with hotel, and transfers. Fishing license are usually included. Fishing tackle and equipment are usually provided. You may have to bring or buy your lures.
3. Jackpot sport fishing charter boats are popular in Quepos Marina Pez Vela. Local fishing areas are about 40 miles offshore. Inshore fishing is available it is cheaper than offshore. Telephone +506-8458-4997 or email info@ jackpotsportfishing.com
4. Papagayo fishing charters Guana caste at the Northwestern corner of Costa Rica. Contact the at Papagayo fishing charters. Or call Captain Fradian at 321-999-6987. They offer half day, or full day charters. You can use PayPal. Rates range from 525 USD to 650 USD the largest boat is 1900 USD.

If you are not sure who to call about fishing charters, try 1-888-414-3474 central American. Great contact for fishing suggestions period the options for fishing are almost endless. Other popular places to fish on the Pacific coast of Costa Rica are Bahia Drake, Playa del Coco, Playa Tamarindo, Jaco, Crocodile Bay, Golito Marina, Los Suenos Marina. Most restaurants Will filet and grill the fish for you for a small fee. you buy the beer amigo! Costa Rica is a fishing paradise. The excitement of the big catch will pump your adrenaline if you are looking for excitement during your trip to Costa Rica! Pura Vida! May you land the Marlin or sailfish amigo!

"Those Who died with the most days fishing, wins."
-Author unknown

Chapter 12

Surfing in Costa Rica

"Once a year go somewhere
you've never been before."
-Dalai Lama

Surfing in Costa Rica. Costa Rica is a popular destination for surfers traveling from all over the world to give the "breaks" a try. The Pacific side seems to have the larger waves and swells. Jaco and Tamarindo are the most popular. Most airlines will accept surfboards when traveling into either San Jose, or Liberia. If not, you can rent a board, or buy a used board which you can resell before departing. Why do people surf? Someone wrote it is because surfing becomes addictive. It is the anticipation of the next big wave. When the wave comes the person has a surge of adrenaline. Most wave rides last only eight seconds. But when you get the big wave it can be five to seven minutes. Therefore, if you want the big wave in Costa Rica you head to the Pacific, and Tamarindo. Not the Caribbean.

Surfing is the "unpredictable reward." When you get the wave, you want you are happier. This quote is from the Inertia. Surfers are looking for the five to seven-foot wave not the three-foot wave. Pavoner on the West coast is known for having the world's second longest break. "Pavoner is in a remote region in the South on the Pacific coast. It is a small beach town and is difficult to visit.

Jaco. South of Tamarindo, in the Central Pacific is the best. Waves here are strong and consistent. It is the home of many surf shops such as Vista Guapa surf camp. You can rent or buy a surfboard here. Jaco is easy to travel and from San Jose.

Witch's Rock. They call this the almost perfect beach break. It is located North in Guanacoste at Santa Rosa and is accessible from Liberia near the Santa Maria Ranger station. Witch's rock is located offshore from Playa Naranjo beach. It is famous for its breaks. Near by is Ollies point also known for its breaks. Witch's is Rock Surf Camp. Located in Tamarindo Costa Rica. A surf camp where the surf is good. Free airport transfer when you fly into Liberia. The package includes hotel stay for 7 nights, and 7 days surfing school with breakfast. There are classes for beginners, intermediate, too advanced. Also, a family package. The owner offers you a free guide when you log on. Telephone 1-877-925-9917. Witchsrocksurfercamp@gmail.com. Prices begin at 930 USD.

Surf camps are Vista Guapa, Surf school of the world, Tortuga Surf camp, Jaco Surf Camp, Room 2 Board. Playa Hermosa is fast developing as a surfing beach. It is in the North near playa del Coco. Sportfishing is also popular. A good place to catch the morning swell. In summary, Costa Rica is a surfer's paradise, and attracts all level of surfers from intermediate to veterans. The waves are big and can make the adrenaline flow. Surfers are important to the tourist economy. There will be a great big welcome sign waiting for you. "Surf is up amigo."

Chapter 13

Arenal and LaFortuna Volcano, Hot Springs, Lake and Waterfall

"Explore, dream, discover."
-Mark Twain

Arenal is known for its famous volcano. When the view is clear you can see a perfect example of a "conical cone" shape at the top. The volcano was active until 2010. Now it occasionally burps or belches gas. I remember my first trip my hotel was at the base. In the night the volcano did a burp and I was awakened from my bed. I quickly ran out into the parking lot for safety. But it was not needed. But it created excitement for me and other visitors. Most people travel to Arenal via LaFortuna, Located on the base of the volcano and its surrounding Lake. It is located 120 miles North of San Jose, or a short flight domestic airline of Nature Air, or Sansa. LaFortuna is a small quiet agricultural town, with hotels, in restaurants. There are boat taxis to Monteverde.

Volcano Arenal activities. Arenal is located near the farming town of LaFortuna. Nearby, his Laguna de Arenal, or Lake Arenal. Adventure Arenal is popular with the tourist. They can organize various tours for you. The volcano is the major reason tourists visit here. They can plan a horse-riding tour, a bike, or a boat tour. Eco guide. This is the largest operator of canopy tours over the rainforest.

Hot Springs. There are numerous Springs in the LaFortuna area. Some are free. Paradise Hot Springs is popular. The hot water is produced by the lava from the volcano. Usually there is a large pool to wade around, and sometimes a waterfall. The water is relaxing. Because of the volcano Arenal has become a popular tourist destination. The tourist has access to the rainforest, waterfalls, Hot Springs, and a large Lake. There are canopy and zip line tours. You came for the adventure, and you will experience it in Arenal.

Arenal: The Volcano and Hot Springs. Arenal is at the top of eco adventure destinations. Here follows a list of popular adventure activities. You will find the rainforest, a lake, a river, waterfalls and the volcano crater. I organized my tour of Costa Rica via the most popular national parks. After touring Manuel Antonio, I go East to see Arenal. The volcano Arenal is formed at the top with a perfect conical shape. Which is rare to see. The volcano is considered "inactive." Most of the time it is difficult to see the cone of the volcano because of the cloud cover. You may not get a good photo. Like Arenal Is at the base of the volcano. It offers hiking trails, and horseback riding. The major town near Arenal is Lafortuna, the home of the hostels, hotels, and various restaurants. The major travel agency is Desafío Adventure Tours telephone+506-2479-0020. www.desafiocostarica.com. You can take a tourist bus, or a taxi boat to LaFortuna on your way to Monteverde. Another major attraction in Arenal are the numerous hot springs. Many are located in conjunction to hotels. There is an abundance of hot thermal springs near the volcano. They are great for soaking the body and rejuvenation after an active day of hiking, or ziplining.

Two of the popular hot springs and Tabacon, or Eco Tamales. Most are only a short drive from LaFortuna. Another major attraction is the Lafortuna waterfall. A must see many tourists visit Costa Rica just to see the numerous waterfalls. There are two observational platforms at Lafortuna falls. There is a free-swimming area. Bring your swimsuit and towel.

Arenal is known for the Arenal Hanging bridges, they are next to the lake. The hanging bridge is a suspension bridge. As you walk across you look down into the rainforest. A great way to get a different perspective of the rainforest to view the canopy and bird life. There are over 200 species of birds. It is a bird watching paradise.

Ziplining the sky trek Is the most popular. The adrenaline will rush as you zip line the canopy with wonderful views of Lake Arenal end of the volcano. You almost feel like you are flying.

Whitewater rafting can be arranged by Desafio Adventures in Lafortuna. The Best is the Rio Sarapiqui Whitewater rafting tour lasting as much as three hours.

Wildlife in Arenal. Three toed sloth- The sloth moves slowly. It sleeps 16 to 18 hours a day. Its habitat is mostly at the Top of the tree canopy. Frogs- frogs prefer to live in the damp and wet cloud forest. The garden frog has disappeared. An unusual frog is the Blue Jean frog, because of its colors. This frog has the ability to change colors or morph. Coati- Related to the raccoon. It is harmless and is not afraid to approach humans. Ocelot- Resembles a home cat in size. It is nocturnal. It is a tree climber. This cat is haunted for its fur. Capuchin Monkey- It has a white face. A common monkey found in Costa Rica. They have large brains and are considered to be smart monkeys. They travel in groups of 40.

National parks of Costa Rica.

Costa rica's dedication to progressive protection of the environment a sustainable ecotourism has led to an inevitable development of national parks system not found in other countries. Currently the country has dedicated 25% Of the land national parks. Manuel Antonio is listed as one of the most beautiful in the world all together, there are 27 parks in Costa Rica you can see the dedication to ecotourism, and why so many tourists each year. The first park was Poas volcano founded in 1925. Other parks range Arenal volcano, to Corcovado. Manuel Antonio, Cahuita park, Guanacaste, Poas, and Tortuguero National park. All are dedicated to the study, and preservation of flora and fauna, and wildlife. Tourism and nature can exist side by side. The people and the government support ecotourism and such sustainability. Nature and the ecosystem must be preserved.

After reading this chapter, it is easy to see that the Arenal park offers the tourist a wide range of tours and cultural insights to the northeastern lowlands of Costa Rica. The volcanoes are the major attraction. The Rapids in zip lines will make the adrenaline flow! so, get out there and enjoy.

Chapter 14

Arenal and LaFortuna Restaurants and Bars Where to eat and sleep

Arenal and LaFortuna Restaurants

The restaurants in these two towns range from inexpensive sodas, or lunch counters, to the expensive sit-down restaurants, found mostly in LaFortuna. The Corner Restaurant and bar located in the middle of Lafortuna, Has a long history here. A favorite of locals, and travelers. Next to the Catholic Church Hwy 142 meets Calle 472. View of the volcano. It is known for its pizza, grilled food, and bar serving wine and beer open daily 6 to 10. Don Rufino. This is probably the best restaurant in Lafortuna. Open for lunch and dinner period price ranges from 14 to 29 USD. It is very popular with the locals. It is located in downtown El Centro LaFortuna. Rufino's Is known for its variety of international foods. They have an indoor grill, and a popular bar. Grilled meats such as ribeye are popular. The menu also has tuna, crab, and chicken. Telephone+506-2479-9997. www.donrufino.com.

Soda Viquez. Breakfast and lunch period server traditional Costa Rican foods at inexpensive soda prices. They offer the traditional cosada and gallo pinto. Very good Hamburgers, and pasta dishes.

Lava Lounge. Attractive bar and drink menu. Attract those who want a cold beer, glass of wine, or rum in Cola laid back atmosphere. The menu includes wraps, and fajitas. At select times they have a broad range. There is coconut chicken, beef, quesilla, sea bass and pork chop cosada. The popular dishes are pizza, sushi, salad, and burgers.

Rainforest Café. Large breakfast. Traditional dishes of cosadas. Calle 1 in Arenal El Centro. Best desserts and pastries. Variety of coffees. Telephone +506-2479-7239.

Soda La Mesa de Mama. The real Costa Rican food such as cosada. Typical inexpensive soda food prepared at the Mesa of Mama. Mama's home cooking. Reasonable prices, good quality food. Authentic. Located in El Castillo. Telephone +506-2479-1954.

Soda La Hormiga. Soda means it is a small cafe. It is located in LaFortuna next to Super Mega. Telephone+506-24799247. Average price is 4 USD. Has great cosada, Grilling and tasty meal. Good service.

Soda La Parada. This sort of cafe is another local favorite in LaFortuna. located in El Centro in front of the bus stop. It is open 24 hours and 7 days. They serve typical Costa Rican food at cheap prices. It is a great place for breakfast either Costa Rican Gallo Pinto or North American. The menu includes hamburgers, La cosada, and typical arroz con, pollo, or shrimp.

One love lounge. Located West of Lafortuna. Just off the main highway near Arenal Oasis lodge just after Arenal Backpackers Resort. It has an unusual outside appearance. If you are of the "hippie" age it looks like the magic bus. They feature live music, especially reggae. Very popular with the locals.

Que Rico Restaurant. LaFortuna In San Carlos. Telephone +506-2479-1020. Italian. Best pizza and pasta. Strong drinks. Located in front of Arenal volcano.

Hotels and Hostels in Arenal and LaFortuna. There are ample places for sleeping ranging in prices from the budget hostel class, to mid-range, and the expensive luxury resort, or lodge.

Backpackers resort. A five-star hostel. Serves Arenal and LaFortuna. Newly renovated and redecorated rooms with great views. The ultimate in relaxation in the center of Arenal. Great view of the Arenal volcano. Hostel has surrounding nature gardens. Bar, pool, and restaurant. Located on Arenal Volcano main road. Three blocks from Central Park towards Arenal volcano, LaFortuna. Telephone +506-2479-7000. Email arenalbackpackersresort@gmail.com. The advertise you will forget it is a hostel. It feels like a resort.

Hotel Finca Luna Nuera Lodge. Arenal volcano. Single rooms 99 USD. Contact info@fincalunanueralodge.com.

Arenal Hostel Resort. Similar to hostel backpackers but are separate hostels. Arenal Hostel has lovely landscaped gardens, and a small pool. Rooms are clean, and well maintained. AC and hot water a beautiful view of the volcano. Located on Ave Central. Telephone +506-2479-9222. www.arenalhostelresort.com. Price range 16 to 58 USD.

Arenal Observatory Lodge and spa. Single price is 115 USD. The only hotel built inside the park. It was originally a research station. It is located just South of base of the volcano. It is considered an upscale hotel, or pricey. The views are stunning. The location is outstanding. It is surrounded by hiking trails, and near a waterfall. The lodge includes a museum, watch is open too only guests of the hotel. Entrance is 8 USD. Pool and Spa. Food is good. You will not be disappointed.Telephone +506-2290-7011. www.arenalobservatorylodge.com

Arenal Volcano Inn. Room rate 76 USD. Located just off the LaFortuna highway toward the Arenal volcano. Great view of Arenal. Constructed as a series of cabins enclosed by a tropical garden. Rooms are large. AC, TV and Wi-Fi. Spacious and clean. Pool, andbreakfast. Peaceful and relaxing. Includes a bar and Italian restaurant. Available activities are hiking, canoeing, horseback riding. Horseback riding is my favorite. Great view and great value.

Chachagua Rainforest Eco Lodge. Telephone +506-4000-2026. LaFortuna Arenal volcano National Park. Chachagua 21007. Single 116 USD. Somewhat secluded near LaFortuna. But a beautiful rainforest experience. Free daily nature walks. Rooms are beautiful, and the food high quality. You are surrounded by nature. This is why you came to Costa Rica. Free Internet, parking, and breakfast included. Pool.

Arenal Park Hotels

Hotel San Bosco. Located in central LaFortuna. This is a budget friendly hotel. AC or fans, TV, Wi-Fi, pool. Only 5km from the Arenal volcano. Single price room 55 USD. Telephone +506-8498-3594.

Hotel Linda Vista. Located in the village El Castillo within 2km of the Arenal. In Spanish Linda Vista means a beautiful view. Clean an affordable. Great location and easy access to the Arenal Eco Zoo, Butterfly observation, end Sky adventure.

Arenal Oasis Ecolodge and Wildlife Refuge. Series, or group of cabins or bungalows each with a front porch and rocking chairs to relax and watch nature all around you. The cabins are spacious and clean. Each cabin has a ceiling fan, TV, and refrigerator. There is a bath or shower. The decor is rustic. They are designed to bring you up close to nature. Literally "nature comes up to your front porch." The average price is 61 USD. Great location and good value. Most have views of Arenal.

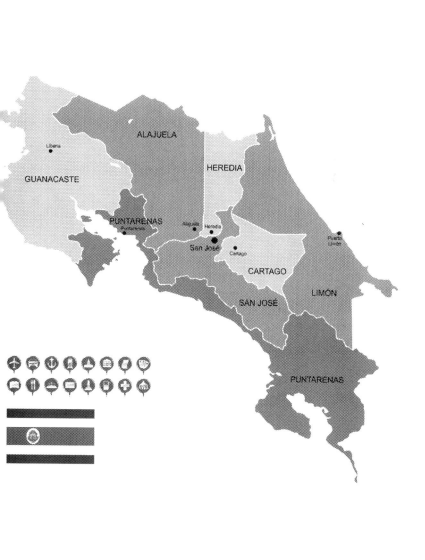

Chapter 15

Monteverde The Cloud Forest

"I haven't been everywhere, but it's on my list."
-Susan Sontag

Monteverde. The next eco adventure is visiting Monteverde, The home of the cloud forest. It is the place you are most likely to see Quetzal, a colorful bird indigenous to Costa Rica. There are numerous frogs, butterflies, and canopy tours. It is a most biodiverse area. Monteverde has the small town of Santa Elena. Nearby is the settlement, and dairy farmers who are Quakers who moved there to find a place to live in peace. The Quaker story is explained elsewhere in this book. It is a truly remarkable story of courage and determination. Monteverde is located a short distance East of LaFortuna and Arenal. DeSafio Tours can arrange a transfer for you. It is about 100 miles North of San Jose. Shuttle buses can be arranged. Another option is to fly on one of the small airlines. You can book with either Sansa or Nature Air. You can hire a boat taxi to cross Lake Arenal.

What to do in Monteverde? Ziplining- This Is the most popular activity. It is said the zip line was invented in Monteverde. You can soar over the cloud forest.

Hanging Bridges-An exciting way to view the canopy.

Night walk- The cloud forest is different at night. You can see nocturnal wildlife such as the sloths.

The butterfly farm- On the road to the entrance gate of Monteverde see the colorful variety of Mariposa, or butterflies.

The hummingbirds- See the daily feeding of the hummingbirds, and educational video.

Hiking in the cloud forest- Look for frogs in the wet damp environment. The Golden frog is now extinct.

Orchids- This flower flourish is in a cloud forest with the ever-present moisture. Also, there is outside the Monteverde gates a commercial orchid garden.

The Quakers- Tour are the dairy farm. Sample the ice cream and cheese.

Bird watching- See the Toucans. If you are lucky you may see the elusive Quetzal.

Mounteverde is a great place to see an abundance of nature and have an adventure.

What is a cloud forest? It is a high-altitude tropical forest that receives much of its moisture from direct contact with clouds rather than rain. Monteverde is a prime example. A rainforest is located at a lower level such as next to the ocean. It receives its moisture from tropical rain. The weather is hot and humid. An example is Manuel Antonio on the Pacific, Tortuguero, on the Caribbean. World climate change could adversely damage the cloud forests. Such as the disappearance of the Golden frog. All of us need to be aware of the potential dangers of climate change. We need to take a stand and make others aware of the dangers.

Monteverde and Santa Elena are both located at the Top of the mountain. Santa Elena is a small town adjacent to Monteverde reserve, the home of the cloud forest. It is the world's most varied ecosystem. This area saw the development of the canopy tours. Hiking is muddy because of the cloud forest. The weather can be cool so bring a light rain jacket. The flora and fauna provide a lush landscape. But the cloud forest is why people travel here. The elevation is 4,400 feet. The Monteverde cloud forest is the richest habitat in the world. It is the best example of ecotourism and biodiversity. Here you can go hiking and ziplining you will see bats, snake's, and frogs. You will learn the basics of the flora and fauna. It is great for birding, but it is difficult to see the elusive Quetzal. It is best to hire A guide. The trails can be muddy when hiking. Overall it was a rewarding experience and I highly recommend a visit to Monteverde. When I first visited, Monteverde I remember visiting the bar Amigos, it was the only bar in town. But a welcome place to visit after a day of activity. I enjoyed meeting the local people and interacting with the culture. I also remember the bumpy dirt road up the mountain. I had a driver and van from San Jose, by the time we arrived back in San Jose my rib cage was aching. But I am glad I made the trip. A footnote for your information. The famous Golden frog is now extinct. You will not see it. The Golden frog disappeared from the environment in 1989. Sadly, it is extinct. It is not sure why. But it has to do with the interaction of the growing human population period perhaps toxins and pesticides? The ecosystem is out of balance? It is just a warning to humans to become more aware of creatures in other environments and to give them equal space to survive. We only have one planet. Let us try to save it.

Chapter 16

Monteverde Hotels and Hostels, Restaurants and Cafes

"When you travel, remember that a foreign country is not designed to make you comfortable. It is designed to make its own people comfortable."
-Clifton Fadiman

Hotels and Hostels in Monteverde. Monteverde and Santa Elena have numerous hotels and Hostels. The price range goes from budget to expensive. Its your choice.

Hotel Poco a poco. Price range 150 USD. Includes a spa, pool, and a restaurant. Family friendly. Upper level rooms have a good view. Rooms are well maintained. Friendly management. Will not disappoint. Includes breakfast. Telephone +506-2645-6000. www.hotel pocoapoco.com.

Monteverde Backpackers. Price range budget 10USD. Lovely wood panel rooms. Comfy rooms. Friendly management. Well maintained rooms range from dorm to private. Located in Santa Elena. Shower with hot water. Free use of the kitchen.

Cloud Forest Lodge. Price range moderate to expensive. 102 USD. Located on a hilltop. You are literally in the clouds. Great view of the forest. Hotel has hiking trails. Bird watching. Lodge consists of private cabins. Can walk to Santa Elena town. Telephone +506-2645-5058.

Sloth Backpackers. Price 40 USD. Located near the bus station in Santa Elena in the center of town. The manager is "Yorle" a friendly and helpful person.

Hotel Bosque. Price 146 USD. Near the cloud forest and the biological reserve. On route 62. Also, near Sky adventures. 1.2 miles From Santa Elena. Free Wi-Fi and free breakfast. Garden and pool can sign up for hiking trails, or a night flash life tour. Bosque means trees.

Mi Casa Tica Hotel. Price 8 USD. The best budget choice. Santa Elena near tourist center, you get a bed in a dormitory. Free breakfast. Backpackers atmosphere. Good for the traveler who is watching spending carefully.

Restaurants and Cafes.

Bar Amigos. Santa Elena and Monteverde. Telephone +506-2645-5071. Popular Bar and Grill in central Santa Elena located near the bank. Popular with locals and tourists. Lots of TV's for sports. Pool tables. Mostly snack food but a reasonable price. Cheap Imperial beer. Live music at night, and sometimes a DJ with karaoke. Dance floor. Food is typical, rice and beans, steak, and nachos.

The Green Restaurant. Specialties in Costa Rican, international, Fusion and health foods. A little pricey, but a good value. Service is good and friendly. Close to town at Plaza Monteverde on the 2nd floor. Telephone +506-2645-7765. Their steaks are the best. They also serve pasta, vegetarian, and a variety of meat skewers. Good selection of wine and beer. Highly recommended.

Sabor Tico Restaurant. This is less expensive. It is a typical Costa Rican restaurant, often called a "soda." It is located next to the soccer field in Santa Elena. You can actually watch a game from the patio. Very popular with locals, or Ticos. The owners and managers are Olman and his wife Yamira. The food is good, and the service is great. Also, good for kids. Telephone +506-2645-5827. A typical Tico meal is of a mixture of rice, beans, meet (steak), salad, in plantains (similar to French fries). This serving is often called a cosada plate. You can also specify fish, or pork instead of beef. A veggie cosada is a alternative for the health conscious vegetarian.

Café Cabure. Specialties in Argentine cuisine such as steaks. Pricey but good service and quality. Also, serves fresh tortilla wraps. The chicken mole is exceptional. Nice patio dining. The owner Susan Salas has brought her unique chocolate making to Monteverde. She makes her own chocolate from the actual bean. She has the best desserts in town. A must see even for a coffee and dessert on the patio to see the sunset. Telephone +506-2645-5020.

Taco Taco. Not expensive, but good value. Basically, it is a takeaway counter in downtown Santa Elena. You can sit on the patio of pension Santa Elena. Large lunch crowd. Taco Taco is your basic Taco stand. Tortilla chips filled with chicken, pork, beef, or fish. Add a slaw in salsa. An ample and filling meal for a budget traveler and a good way to meet people.

Sofia Restaurant. An upscale option. They offer a Latin America Fusion menu. They have a modern Latin menu. Price 20 USD. They use traditional ingredients. Great cocktail bar.

Chapter 17

The Story of the Quakers in Monteverde

"Wherever you go, go with all your heart."
-Confucius

The Quakers in Monteverde is a fascinating story of dedication to their religious beliefs, and the perseverance to overcome all odds to follow their beliefs. They came from Fairhope Alabama just outside of Mobile after World War two, and prior to the Korean war. That Quakers are pacifists and were opposed to the war. Some had spent time in jail because of their beliefs. They set out on a journey to find a place they could live in peace and pursue their beliefs. They found it in Costa Rica where the citizens had abolished the army. Some people offered to sell them some land on the top of Monteverde where the Quakers set up a dairy farms. They could produce and sell dairy products such as milk and cheese. They built schools which were so highly rated even the locals preferred to send their children there if they were accepted academically. They had an important impact on the economy of Monteverde. The Quakers had found their home!

Chapter 18

Tortuguero Park "The Amazon of Costa Rica."

"Do not follow where the path may lead.
Go instead where there is no path and leave a trail."
-Ralph Waldo Emerson

Tortuguero National park was founded in 1975, and is located in the Limon region, or the providence in the remote North Eastern part of Costa Rica. Bing a remote region, it can best be reached by airplane or boat. San Jose is about three hours away by land travel. A bus from San Jose can take you partially to the outskirts of the park. The park today is the third most visited park. The park takes its name from the turtle and is located on the Caribbean Ocean.

The name Tortuguero means the land of the "turtles." Because of the annual migration of the Green Sea turtle to the beaches of Tortuguero once a year to lay eggs, or nest. It is a moving experience for the tourists, and the volunteers who serve to count the population. The nesting season runs from March to October. The Green turtles are most active In July and August. Leather neck turtles arrive in April. To view this annual event, you must have a certified guide to be sure the Turtles can peacefully perform this biological process. The turtle, using some internal instinct or "radar" makes the trip once a year, sometimes traveling 5000 miles. They have been tracked using radio beepers reports National Geographic Television.

The largest city on the Caribbean East coast of Costa Rica is Puerto Limon. This sea port became popular in the 19th century when banana and coffee exports ruled the country. Limon played an important role in the founding of United Fruit Company.

Today cruise ships arrive here. Plans are being made to build a large container port. The turtle population is in danger of losing numbers and must be saved. There are several nonprofit organizations working with volunteers for this purpose. A popular organization is the Sea Turtle Conservancy who have research stations in Tortuguero. They have a visitor center and museum. It is located just North of Tortuguero village. The peak season for tourists is July and August. The best way to explore Tortuguero is by boat with a guide. Because the Tortuguero National Park is surrounded by a network, or maze of canals. You explore the park and look for wildlife by boat. The rainforest is dense and therefore too thick to explore by foot. The amount of rain contributes to its biodiversity. As the boat quietly floats down the River canals you will see birds, snakes, monkeys and perhaps the endangered Jaguars. Some call it the "Amazon" of Costa Rica because of the Rivers and the maze of canals. The River and canals, located North of Limon, flow Parallel to the Caribbean ocean. The turtles lay their eggs on the sand beaches. The beaches are wonderful for walking. The waves and undertow make the ocean too dangerous for swimming. An early morning canal boat trip is the best time to spot wildlife with your guide. Each boat tour is two to three hours. Be sure to have a hat and rain gear. Always use sunscreen. The village of Tortuguero is a very small town with only a few restaurants, souvenir stores and small hotels. It is probably best to pre book your tour, and hotel in San Jose. You will then have coordinated transportation and transfers, and a guaranteed hotel or lodge with a guide waiting for you. Costa Rica Expeditions in San Jose is an example of a tour agency who can book the entire trip for you. This includes transportation, transfers, and hotels with activities. Costa Rica experts is another travel tour agency from San Jose who can book an entire trip for you. They have 30 years of experience. www.costaricaexperts.com.

Chapter 19

Hotels and Hostels in Tortuguero

"Two roads diverged in a wood and I – I
took the one less traveled by."
-Robert Frost

Hotels and where to sleep in Tortuguero.

Aracari Garden Hostel. Budget class. 31 USD. Telephone +506-2767-2240 in CR. Free Wi-Fi, fans. Shared kitchen. Lounge for relaxation. A nice serene garden. Near the park and a short walk to the beach. Located South of the Futbol field. Lockers for storage and safety. Dorm for mixed gender. Bunk beds.

Riverview Hotel. Telephone +506-8579-9414. Price 41 USD. Free Wi-Fi. Great view of the River, or canal. AC. Restaurant on ground floor. Clean and a friendly staff.

Tortuga Lodge and Gardens. The lodge is owned and operated by Costa Rica Expeditions in San Jose. Price 74-220 USD. Upscale. Beautiful wooden building. Attractive landscaping. Excellent view facing the River. Has restaurant and bar. Near the airstrip. They have their own boats and guides. Clean and well maintained. I booked this Hotel and wildlife boat safari. They made all the arrangements and transfers. It was somewhat pricey, but they took care of all the details. They are a very good company. A great trip!

La Casona. Telephone +506-2709-8092. Price 25 USD. Lovely garden. Kitchenette. Near the futbol field. Clean and well maintained.

Hotel Miss Junie. Moderate price. 50 USD. Includes breakfast. The upstairs rooms have a nice view of the canal. The grounds are well developed and an attractive tropical look. Great for relaxing. The building reminds you of a Caribbean plantation. Staff is friendly. Clean and well maintained. Attached restaurant. Hotel is located on Main Street at the North End toward the park.

Tour Companies.

There are many selections for tours. One is Pachira Lodge Tortuguero canal tour. Remember, the gate entrance fee is separate from the tour. The Pachira Lodge USA Telephone 1-866-853-9426. The lodge reservations can be reached at Google, Trip Advisor, or Pacific Trade Winds. Also, try www.costarica.com/

tours/Tortuguero.com. They can arrange fishing trips as well. Remember, don't forget a Tortuguero Turtle tour. This is why most people travel here.

Another popular tour company is Willies Tours Costa Rica. Telephone +506-2725-1024, or +506-8917-6982. They are located in Cahuita.

Cahuita village was founded by an Afro-Caribbean settler in 1828. It is adjacent to Playa Negra, a dark sandy beach. If you stay overnight in Cahuita the Alby Lodge, owned by a German is recommended. Price 60 USD. It has beautiful landscaped grounds. There are birds and howler monkeys. Willies Tours offers a night life tour of Cahuita for 35 USD. It is a bar hopping tour. Willies has transfers from San Jose and Lafortuna.

What to do in Tortuguero.

Sea Turtle tours. Turtle watching is what brings most tourists to Tortuguero. The peak season is July-September. Green Turtles nest at this time. You will need a trained guide. Other turtles are the Leathernecks, Hawksbill, and Loggerhead.

Boat tours. You will need to take a jungle boat safari to travel the maze of canals with a guide. Tortuguero has an abundance of wildlife. It is biodiverse. Monkeys are easy to spot. there are white faced, howler, and spider. The two toed sloth as well. Green McCaw and Toucans. Over 300 bird species.

Hiking. The El Gavillian trail is most popular. Starts at the southern end of town at the Rangers station and weaves through the rain forest.

Sportfishing. Snook and Tarpon fishing is the most popular. There are half day trips, or the more expensive full day trips. Just visit the docks and ask questions.

Visit a Village. Get to know the people and the culture. Perhaps buy a souvenir.

Sea Turtle Conservancy center. There is a welcome center and museum. Located North of Tortuguero town. Free movie about wildlife. Information about conserving the sea turtle. Cost 2 USD.

Biologist Archie Carr. Carr was born in Mobile Alabama USA. His area of study were the sea turtles and its habitat. To learn more, he traveled to the Caribbean more specifically Tortuguero. He found there was overharvesting and a decline in the numbers of sea turtles especially the green sea turtle. His plan was to work together with the local population to educate and promote conservation.

Tortuguero National Park.
"Adventure is worthwhile."
-Aristotle

Tortuguero. Why visit Tortuguero National Park. Tortuguero Stands out in contrast to the other parks. It is an "Amazon" maze of dense rainforest and winding canals. You explore the park by boat. It rains frequently which contributes to its rich biodiversity. You view the animal life in flora and fauna by floating down the peaceful canals. You will see exotic birds, and hear the howling monkeys, and often see the large snakes hanging from the branches of trees. You will need a certified guide. Tortuguero is famous for its green sea turtles who lay their eggs here to hatch. You can volunteer to help save the turtles, and therefore have a chance to adopt an endangered sea turtle. Not many people get to have this experience. It is because you care about our planet. Climate change is real!

Chapter 20

Restaurants and Cafes in Tortuguero

"The more you travel, the less you realize you know."
-Anthony Bourdain

Tortuguero is a small town. There is not much in the way of nightlife. You can always drink at your hotel or lodge. July is the peak turtle season. Otherwise you can go to the town and have dinner at.

Taylor's place. The owner is Ray Taylor. Price is inexpensive. 7 USD. They specialize in grilled fish. Grilled fish in a garlic sauce is the specialty. Serve alcohol. Nice garden setting. Located South of the fubol, or soccer field. Well established and popular.

Miss Junies. Moderate price. 15 USD. Serves Caribbean food. Fish, chicken, lobster are popular menu selections. Serves Costa Rican rice and beans. Very well-known and popular with locals and tourists alike. Located on North Main Street. You can't go wrong.

Budda Café. Inexpensive to moderate. 12 USD. Specializes in pizza and crepes. A relaxing River setting. some tables are outside. Vegetarian options available.

Wild Ginger. Moderate prices. 12-24 USD. Serves lobster, ceviche, and Caribbean beef Stew. Located in the North. On a dirt Rd near the school and sea turtle conservancy center. Also, has hamburgers for the Norte Americanos. It's unnoticed by many tourists.

Soda Dona Maria. This is the typical Costa Rican soda, or small café. The prices are budget class. It offers the cosada, sandwiches, and burgers. There are juices, colas, beer and wine. It is near the entrance to the park.

For music and alcoholic drinks try La Calebra near the public river? They serve up music and beer.

Now it is time to say goodbye to the fascinating Tortuguero park and its wildlife along with the turtles. It has been a trip to never forget. Such a beautiful jungle and rainforest! But before we reluctantly say goodbye, we reflect upon my trip Costa Rica and its National Parks. I started in San Jose, a wonderful Spanish colonial city. Then on to Manuel Antonio and the pacific beach. Next inland to Arenal volcano. From there to Monteverde and the cloud Forest Next, Tortuguero and the canals, and the turtles were the next highlight of my ecoadventure. Costa Rica has the most stable democracy in Latin America. The people are happy. It has been called the "Switzerland of Central America." (Molina) The Quakers selected Monteverde for a place to live. You can travel the world, but you will find no other country has made concerted and concerned effort to protect the environment as have the people of Costa Rica. Costa Rica is a leader in the ecotourism movement.

Costa Rica is concerned about global warming. The country is concerned about deforestation. They are doing their best to protect the forest and replant the rainforests. The National Park systems of Costa Rica is a prime example. To sum up my trip to Costa Rica. You will see exotic birds and wildlife, hike in the jungle rainforest and mountain cloud forests. See volcanos, visit hot springs, take a boat cruise on the canals of Tortuguero, and relax on beaches. A trip of a lifetime.

Pura Vida Amigo!
John P. Cross

Remember we have only one planet.
Take care of it!

Earth Matters

Don't mess with Mother Nature!

"Perhaps travel cannot prevent bigotry but by demonstrating that all people cry, laugh, eat, worry, and die, it can introduce the idea that if we try and understand each other, we may even become friends."
-Maya Angelou

Once you visit Costa Rica you realize how beautiful nature is to each of us. The importance of saving and sustaining the environment is apparent. More so now since we have wasted too much time. The earth does matter. The tree population in Costa Rica, and elsewhere in Brazil are most important. The trees play a role of carbon exchange watch in return causes rainfall. We must not support deforestation. The loss of trees causes climate change. It causes ice melting in Greenland, The Arctic, end and Antarctica. The oceans rise and we lose valuable ocean beaches. In Bali I found the ocean reefs were disappearing. Plastics dumped into the ocean is a major problem. Some birds, fish, or turtles consume the objects, and they die.

In Tanzania Africa I found that the Mt. Kilimanjaro snows, and ice cap are slowly melting because of climate change. In China and India auto pollution is making it difficult to breathe. Last time in China I accumulated particles of dark smoke in my nose. Just before the Olympics in China they planted trees to help improve the quality of the air period, but it was only a temporary solution. On my last trip to China it was almost impossible to take photos of the forbidden Kingdom buildings because of the thick pollution. Air pollution cause affect the destruction of historic buildings. Coal is used to produce electricity. Great progress has been made in the use of solar power. This trend must continue. Solar power is cheap and clean. Windmills are an alternative. You will find them in Holland and out West in the USA. Time is a factor in environmental recovery. The people of the world need to recognize action must be taken. Time and the climate waits for no one.

Save the planet!
John Cross

Final Words

Why I Travel?

"Man cannot discover new oceans unless he
has the courage to lose sight of the shore."
-Andre Gide

Travel is my passion. My first major trip was to Mexico City, one of my favorite cities. I saw museums, colonial architecture, and the great pyramids to the Aztec sun and moon gods. The travel "bug" got me and continues to motivate me to explore the world. My college studies of history, geography, and languages have contributed to my motivation to travel. Later after a trip to Quebec City, I took my first trip to Europe. I was impressed by the old-world charm of museums, history, and architecture, such as you find in Paris, Rome, and Florence. Travel and learning became an obsession it would not let go. I was hooked forever on travel. Travel is a University in itself. One never stops learning. The adventure never ends. Just give me an airline ticket, I am happy.

By this time, I had received my Master's degree in history. History, along with traveling and learning was my passion. I also learned to travel on a budget, And I integrate budget ideas into my books. If you can dream it you can do it. my greatest travel accomplishment was climbing Mount Kilimanjaro. I still love Africa especially Kenya and Tanzania, where I travel frequently.

I have traveled to all seven continents of the world. Antarctica was special to see. The polar bears of the Canadian Arctic made a lasting impression. Traveling the trans-Siberian railroad from Beijing, to Mongolia, across Siberian to Moscow and St. Petersburg ranks high on my most enjoyable lists. A must see is the Hermitage museum in St. Petersburg. I was in Berlin. Just after the wall came down how exhilarating it was to see history being made. I shall never forget. I have pieces of the wall at home. Travel is my goal in life! But my travels almost came to an end in 2009 while try traveling in Patagonian in Chile during the winter. I slipped on some ice and snow and had a severe break of my right ankle. It took six operations over a span of two years to repair the ankle. It was followed by rehabilitation. Today I walk with a cane, but the ankle will never be normal. However, I continue to travel, but I will no longer be climbing mountains. My motto is "just go!"

Top 10 reasons I travel

1. Travel opens your eyes to a larger view of the world.
2. Learn a new language and enjoy a new culture.
3. Adventure and excitement. For the fun of it.
4. Education. Travel is a University where you can learn firsthand what you cannot learn in a classroom. Travel is an education.
5. Make a dream come true. See Egyptian pyramids or the Taj Mahal in India.
6. Stories to tell for the rest of your life or write travel books.
7. Sample new exotic foods such as grilled grasshoppers in Zimbabwe.
8. Prove to yourself that you can. You can climb Mount Kilimanjaro or trek the mountain trails of the Himalayans in Nepal. It is a challenge and sense of accomplishment.
9. See the environment firsthand. See the monkeys and bird of Costa Rica or the lion and cheetah in Tanzania or Kenya. The polar bears of the Arctic or the Penguins of Antarctica. The migrating whales of Baja Mexico. Sea turtles being released into the ocean in Baja and the Caribbean off the coast of Costa Rica.
10. To find yourself. Just as The Beatles traveled to India. Find the meaning to your life. Everyone has a reason to travel.

You have seen my reasons for travel. I will
continue to travel. Just Go! Pura Vida!
"If you do not have a story to tell
then you have never traveled."
-John P. Cross, Author

Appendix 1: Packing checklist/ Travel check list

"When preparing to travel, layout your clothes
and all your money for the upcoming trip. Then
take half the clothes and twice the money."
-Susan Heller

Items to pack

- Passport & visa. Make sure it is up to date and not ready to expire.
- Airline tickets and vaccination certificate.
- Travel insurance
- Prescriptions
- Mini first aid kit
- Toiletries
- Toilet paper
- Soap and shampoo
- Sunscreen and sunglasses
- Electrical adapters and converters

- Face cloth
- Mini detergent
- Alarm clock
- Camera and memory cards, or film
- Battery, and charger

Appendix 2: Basic Spanish for travel and Costa Rica slang

"If you talk to a man in a language he understands,
that goes to his head. If you talk to him in
his own language, that goes to his heart.
-Nelson Mandela

The best way to learn Spanish, or any language, is to ask questions. Your understanding of a language and cultural awareness goes a log way in making friends and negotiating the price of a souvenir, or artifact. Just try! Don't be afraid. Your efforts will be appreciated. Use "Donde esta" as an easy way to ask a question. Donde esta (bano) (ATM) (Hotel) or Un Mas Cerveza. You may decide that you need a Spanish tutor before you travel to learn enough basic vocabulary and phrases, and to ask a questions. Your trip will be more meaningful if you do. Learn a new language and enjoy a new country, a new culture and your trip.

Rosetta stone language course is an excellent way to learn a second language. Contact www.rosettastone.

com. They offer CD's and a mobile app. You can hear the native accents as well. For a reference use Collins, Spanish Concise Dictionary, 3rd Harper Collins, NYC, USA, 2006. Another way to study is to use Babbel at www.babel.com. Babbel has apps which are compatible with the iphone, tablet, and the PC. I tried it with my PC. They offer a thirty-day free course to see if you like it. You can use Babbel to translate on the go, or home. It is easy and fun to use. Babbel is similar to playing a computer game.

Congnates makes it easier to learn Spanish. Congnates are words in two languages which have a similar spelling and a similar meaning. Spanish has many congnates which relate, or similar to English words. Some examples are accidente or accident, and decider, or decide. Similar words in Spanish and English make learning and retention faster.

Basic Spanish for Travel

Greetings

Yes-Si
No-No
Hello-Hola
Goodbye-Adios
Please-Por Favor
Gracias-Thank you
Pardon me-Perdon
Good morning-Buenos Dias
Good Afternoon- Buenos Tardes
Good night- Buenos Noches
Thank you very much- Muchas Gracias
You're Welcome- De Nada
Excuse me- Conpermiso
I'm sorry- Lo Siento

Questions

What's up? - Que Tal
How are you? - Como estas

What is your name? - Mi Nombre
Where is the? - Donde esta
The toilet or bathroom. - Bano
I am hungry. - Tengo hambre
I am thirsty. - Tengo sed
what time is it? - Que hora es
Why? - Porque
How much? - Quanto
No Entiendo- I don't understand
How do you say in Spanish? - Como sedice
Do you speak English? - Hablas Ingles
Malo-Bad
Need a doctor- Necesito um medico
Police- Policia
On sale- Hay Descuentas
I like it! - Me Gusta
How much? - Cuanto cuesta
Pay with card- Con tarjeta
SJO- San Jose International Airport
CR- Costa Rica

Restaurants

Menu-El menu, or lista
The bill please-La cuenta por favor
I would like- Megusta
Beer please-Una cerveza
Typical food- Comida Tipica
Fish soup in a marinde-Cerriche
Desert-Posthes

Steak-Beef steak, carne, or carne de
Cerdo-Pork
Fish-Pescador
Shrimp-Camaton
Pollo-Chicken
Tenderloin steak- Carne asada
Comida-To eat or meals
Rice-Arroz
I want-Quiero
Breakfast-Eldesayuno
Lunch-Almuerzo
Dinner-Cena
Good-Bueno
Check How much-La Quenta
To drink-Berbida

Finance

ATM-Cajero automatic
Bank-El banco
Exchange rate, or to make a money exchange-Combio

Phrases

Greetings, Life is good. Enjoy, or
how is it going-Pura Vida!
It has been my pleasure-Con mucho gusto
Goodbye-Chao

Costa Rican slang Spanish

Spanish is the second most popular language in the world, after English. Words, idioms, phrases can differ in Spanish speaking countries. Sometimes you must learn specific "slang" in a Latin country. That is the case with Costa Rica. Here are some of my favorite "slang" vocabulary in Costa Rica so that you will not be caught by complete surprise.

Tico- This is not exactly a slang word. It has become widely accepted because it is in constant use. A Tico is someone who is from Costa Rica. The local newspaper is called the Tico Times.

Pura Vida- This is another popular saying in Costa Rica. Pura Vida means "the pure life." Also, it can mean "life is good." It is a popular greeting. It can mean "what's up?" Que Tal in mexico is "what's up?"

Mae- Means friends, or a friend. Or bro or dude.

Tuanis- Cool or awesome. Ok

Detras del palo- Unique to CR. Behind the tree, or he does not know what's going on. Out of touch.

Birra- Beer

Goma- Hangover

Al Chile- Seriously?

Chunche- Means a object, or thing you cannot name.

Brete- Slang for work.

Cosada-A Costa Rican meal using rice, black beans, plantains, salad, and a tortilla and an optional entrée chicken, beef, pork, fish etc. Locals called the ingredients "married" because they go together.

Gallo Pinto- A side dish of rice and beans. Often served with eggs for breakfast.

Bibliography

Molina and palmer, The History of Costa Rica. 2nd ED. San Jose. University of Costa Rica press 2007.

Kaiser, Costa Rica. Ecoadventures in Paradise. 2nd ED. Destinations press 2016.

Cohen, Rich. The Fish that ate the Whale: The Life and Times of America's Banana King. 2013. Picades press.

Chapman, Peter. Bananas: How the United Fruit Company shaped the world. Cannon Gate press. Edinburgh, Scotland UK. 2009

Kohnston, Lonely Planet, Costa Rica Spanish Phrasebook and Dictionary, 2017. Melbourne.

Gabat, Michael. Empire by Invitation: William Walker and Manifest Destiny in Central America, Harvard U. press, 2018.

Toft, Catherine and Wright, Timothy. Parrots of wild. Berkley. U California press, 2015.

Haker, Intro to cloud Forest Trees Monteverde, Costa Rica, 2nd ED, Revised & updated 2000 Mountain Gem Publications, USA.

Forshaw, Joseph. Parrots of the World. Princeton Field Guide. Princeton U. press. 2010 NJ.

Garrigaoles, Richard, The Birds, A Field Guide of Costa Rica. Zona Tropical Publishers, Barnes and Noble, USA,2014.

Reid, Fiona, The Wildlife of Costa Rica. Zona Tropical publishers, Cornel U. press, Ithaca, NY. USA. 1955.

Ortez, Willie. Animals of Costa Rica: Journey into the Rainforest. Creative space books. FLA. USA.2016.

Kahler, Frommer's Costa Rica, 2017 Frommers Publishers. NYC. USA

Kaiser, James. Costa Rica: The Complete Guide; Ecotourism in Costa Rica 215. Destination press. USA

Fodor's Costa Rica. Internet Brands. El Segundo, CA. USA.

Buettner, Dan. National Geographic: The search for Happiness. Nov. 2017. Washington, D.C. USA. Vol.232, No.5.

Kohnstam, Thomas. Lonely Planet Costa Rican Spanish Phrasebook and Dictionary, Melbourne. 2017.

McKibben, Bill. Falter, 2018. Random House, NYC, USA.

Simpson, William. The Best Places for Fishing in North and Central America: Fishing & Traveling around the world. 2011, Kindle Amazon press.

Parise, Mike. Surfers Guide to Costa Rica

Index

Printed in the United States
By Bookmasters